Table of Contents

P9-BZU-265

A Note from the Editor

Self-esteem is a powerful source of emotional energy that can guide us to accomplish great things and overcome significant obstacles. However, it is sometimes an elusive concept. Is it something we are born with? Is it something we develop and cultivate from our experiences and choices? Or, is it both?

My own search for a better understanding of self-esteem led me to a revelation that the variety of definitions for self-esteem parallels the variety of individuals writing the definition—and those seeking that definition. Self-esteem is about self (the individual). Since we are all unique in our individuality, we will also be unique in how we choose to view self-esteem and how that view affects our lives.

The Life and Business coaches who have contributed to this book reinforced that understanding. These chapters offer 12 views about what self-esteem is, how it affects our lives, and what we can do with our awareness of its impact on ourselves, those people dear to us, and the world we touch.

The chapters are organized to flow from chapter to chapter. However, the content is such that you can start with those sections you are most drawn to. Putting the suggestions that are presented into practice will help you change your perspective of who you are and what you want for your life. I highly recommend reading the content more than once, as you will find new nuggets of information each time that you do.

Developing your self-esteem and self-worth is a journey to knowing and appreciating your self better. Strength and confidence come from within. Trust your heart, live your life's dreams, and enjoy your journey!

Marilyn Schwader, Editor

Acknowledgements

Self-esteem begins with love. I am blessed and grateful to have an abundance of people who love me for all of who I am. Thank you to my family for encouraging me to dream big and for your unending belief in my abilities to accomplish those dreams. Thank you to my friends for being my mirrors, and for reminding me of my capabilities. And a very special thank you to all of the coaches who contributed to this compilation. I am very grateful for the opportunity to work with such an incredible gathering of experience, knowledge, and talent.

Marilyn Schwader, Editor

Foreword

by Marcia Reynolds, M.A., M.Ed., M.C.C.

If you could compare your inner world to the solar system, clearly your self-esteem is the sun, with all other aspects of your self revolving around it. How light, how dark, how warm, or how cold your life feels directly relates to the strength of your self-esteem. Many psychologists work with this model, declaring that personal happiness, relationships, achievement, success, creativity, and even sex lives revolve around one characteristic: self-esteem. Deep inside, you carry an image of who you are and how worthy you are in relation to others. One life event after another can change your perception of who you are. Whether or not that perception actually corresponds to reality, this image affects everything from what clothes you wear to your choices of spouse and career.

You arrive in this world with everything needed to feel valued and unique. But, in the course of your life, layers are added that create a complex internal representation. The result is a framework for the way you carry out your life. If the layers are deep, that framework is not easily altered.

Therefore, to stay healthy, caring for your self-esteem with the same commitment that you care for your body is critical. Without a sense of self-worth, you cannot take the risks and make decisions that are necessary to lead a fulfilling and productive life. A lack of self-esteem affects all the parts of your life: career, family, love, and most important, your internal sense of well being. Having self-esteem brings confidence, assertiveness, and the ability to problem-solve. A strong sense of self-worth creates a type of self-fulfilling prophecy: when you like yourself, you begin to act in likable ways; the more belief you have in your ability to achieve, the more likely it is that you will.

The good news is that you can improve your self-esteem. The first step is to recognize that you have choices: you can either let your self-doubts control your actions, or you can work to improve the things you can change and accept those you can't. Despite the layers to your self-image, you are capable of stripping away the negative ones and replacing them with positive ones.

If you are ready to do whatever it takes to change your relationship with your self, this book offers invaluable ideas and insights from Life and Business Coaches as a guide to increasing your self-esteem. From reshaping the past to orchestrating the future, from living from the inside out to creating an outside that supports your inner self, from learning to love to loving to learn, this book is an important collection of tools to help you feel your life is shining brightly.

If you want to have a healthier, stronger relationship with your self and others, to fulfill your potential, and to trust what your own heart is telling you, I strongly recommend that you take the words presented in these chapters to heart. When you reaffirm your sense of worth, you'll rise in the eyes of the most important person—yourself.

Marcia Reynolds, M.A., M.Ed.

Marcia is a Master Certified Coach, Past President, International Coach Federation, and the author of *How to Outsmart Your Brain*, a book that teaches how to channel the power of emotions to forge strong relationships, reap financial rewards, and increase the joyous noise of laughter in people's lives. Read more at www.covisioning.com.

Expressing Your Distinctive Self

by Schuyler Morgan

"ALL PEOPLE ARE THE SAME.
IT IS ONLY THEIR HABITS THAT ARE DIFFERENT."
~ CONFUCIUS ~

How can it be that some people have so many real and subjective advantages? The answer is found partially in their idea of self—their own verdict about their likeability, their competence, their "powerfulness" or ability to handle life. In other words, the answer rests in their self-esteem. People who like themselves allow themselves to succeed in all aspects of life.

Self-esteem is the sense of knowing what and who we are. Having a sense of self gives us the courage to live out a very personal knowledge of ourselves in our daily actions, choices, and way of interacting with the world. With this knowledge, our self-trust, and most important, our self-respect increases.

People with high self-esteem have many advantages when it comes to choosing their right livelihoods. Thus, it is helpful to examine the critically important skills and characteristics that such individuals share. This chapter about expressing your distinctive self brings some legendary principles to life, giving them a voice, revealing their secrets, and explaining how they come to be such preeminent elements in the foundation and structure of self esteem. The following three principles have been my guide and inspiration for an empowered and fulfilling life. I hope that you, too, will find them helpful on your journey of self-esteem.

- The Belief System Called "Myself"
- Treating Yourself As If You Count
- Finishing Up – The Finishing Touches to Express Your Distinctive Self.

The Belief System Called Myself

"THE CHOICES YOU MAKE AS YOU CREATE YOUR OWN IMAGE CAN,
IF WELL CHOSEN, TRANSMIT A VERY POSITIVE STATEMENT ABOUT YOU
AND WHAT YOU THINK ABOUT YOURSELF."
~ SCHUYLER MORGAN ~

One day a naturalist who was passing by a farm saw in the barnyard a flock of chickens, and among them was an eagle. The naturalist inquired of the owner why it was that an eagle, the king of all birds, should be reduced to living in the barnyard with the chickens.

"Since I have given it chicken feed and trained it to be a chicken, it has never learned to fly," replied the owner. "It behaves as chickens behave, so it no longer thinks of itself as an eagle."

"Still," insisted the naturalist, "it has the heart of an eagle and can surely be taught to fly."

After talking it over, the two men agreed to find out whether this was possible. Gently, the naturalist took the eagle in his arms and said, "You belong to the sky and not to the earth. Stretch forth your wings and fly."

The eagle, however, was confused; he did not know who he was. Seeing the chickens eating their food, he jumped down to be with them again.

Undismayed, the naturalist took the eagle up on the roof of the house and urged him again, saying, "You are an eagle. Stretch forth your wings and fly." But the eagle was afraid of his unknown self and the world and jumped down once more for the chicken food.

On the third day, the naturalist rose early and took the eagle out of the barnyard to a high mountain. There he held the king of the birds high above him and encouraged him again, saying, "You are an eagle. You belong to the sky as well as the earth. Stretch forth your wings now and fly!"

The eagle looked back towards the barnyard and up to the sky. Still he did not fly. Then the naturalist lifted him straight towards the sun, and it happened: the eagle began to tremble; slowly he stretched his wings. At last, with a triumphant cry he soared into the heavens. [*]

[*] This story and theme were adapted from Jerry Fankhauser's excellent books, *From a Chicken to an Eagle* and *The Way of the Eagle*.

The eagle in this story represents our true identity as beings of unlimited power and potential. The chicken represents the part of our mind that is earthbound by fear, limitation, and the conditioned boundaries that others have suggested to us—and to which we have agreed.

What are the factors that influence our belief system? What shapes us and makes us who we are? At times, it seems possible that we have all been genetically, biologically, and hormonally "preprogrammed" to behave in certain ways ("it's our nature"). While there is a good measure of truth to this—the bio-behavioral factors may form a foundation for our proclivities—they are not the only factors that influence who we ultimately become as adults, and what we do. We cannot discount the importance of our society and upbringing in our behavior as individuals; those aspects are essential to the development of our belief system of who we are, how we are to be, and our self-esteem.

From the moment we were tiny infants, our families (by their modeling behavior and direct intervention), as well as our society (in school, through religious customs and beliefs, from the media, and so on) have taught us to act in certain "acceptable" ways. This is called social learning or socialization. So, we abide by certain mutually agreed-upon rules that we have imposed on ourselves for our own good and the good of the community.

A family is a form of community, and every family has its own private standards of behavior. Some are overtly verbalized ("There's a long tradition of going to law school in the Smith family! No child of mine is leaving the house in that kind of outfit!"). Others are simply implied or unconsciously acted upon.

Taken together, these societal and familial rules transform us from masses of quivering protoplasm into human beings that function in our society. Limits and rules vary from family to family, region to region, culture to culture, but they exist everywhere that people encounter others. Though they may differ dramatically from one society to the next, all societies and families in the world share the need to establish certain conventions. These conventions primarily concern the following areas: aggression and passivity; sexuality and sex role identity; dependence and independence; emotional development and attachment to others; cooperation and competition; sense of individuality and community; right and wrong; and concrete living experiences such as eating, working, cleanliness, attire, habitat, education, pain, birth, death, and so on.

Other rules and conventions that shape how we behave are more hidden. Gender identity is an important part of the unchanging core of our personalities, and it develops early. Children learn how boys and girls "ought to" act from the way their parents, caregivers, and teachers treat them; by observation of adult behavior; and through peer pressure, television, magazines, and movies. These factors leave indelible impressions that we carry with us into adulthood.

For example, whether or not male and female infants actually act differently, in our society we treat them quite differently from the moment we wrap them in their little blue or pink receiving blankets right after delivery. Social psychologists studying sex role development have found that because of this kind of disparate treatment throughout childhood, girls are taught to be fragile, dependent, compliant, cooperative, and nurturing; whereas boys learn to be sturdy, independent, active, assertive, aggressive, and unemotional.

Children learn not just from their parents and family, but from nursery rhymes, fairy tales, cartoons, television shows, movies, stories, video/internet games, newspapers, magazines, and books. When most of us were growing up, more often than not, the underlying theme in these various cultural influences was that the females should be sweet, kind, and good, and the males were the beasts and bullies.

Contemporary media are filled with images of good and bad boys and girls. Powerful female role models have seeped into our culture with characters that influence us like Buffy the Vampire Slayer and Xena the Warrior Princess who have far exceeded the Wonder Woman's legacy. This is a far cry from the passivity of the Sleeping Beauty of yesteryear.

However, despite this more gender-equal, pop-culture bent, if you conducted an informal survey of youngsters' Halloween costumes, you would still find a lot of little girls dressed as fairy princesses or ballerinas decked out in tutus, and boys dressed as pirates, devils, soldiers, firemen, and cowboys. The culture is giving double messages.

In spite of all our upbringing and influences, as we enter the new millennium there are more women than ever in the workforce, in positions of power, being elected to public office, and playing central roles in major industries. We admire those who are at the very apex of their careers, women who have beaten the odds and remained ladies along the way. Our most-admired Hollywood star is not a male action hero but the genteel leading lady Julia Roberts. Our number-one talk show host, Oprah Winfrey, is not a sleaze peddler but a paragon of compassion and social consciousness. And two of the best athletes in the world are teenage sisters Venus and Serena Williams—women who have revived the game of tennis with a combination of strength, grace, and style.

Aside from their remarkable achievements, these women also shine for the way they conduct themselves in many aspects of their lives—with grace, dignity, and a constant awareness of how their behavior impacts others. They're living proof that how we succeed is just as important as success itself.

In our culture today, we place an increasingly high premium on professional success, earthly possessions, and outward appearance—at almost any price. The media gives us what we allegedly want: stories ad nauseam about celebrities' new looks, new mansions, new lovers, and trips to rehab and jail. And let's not forget those chart-topping TV shows like *Who Wants to Marry a Millionaire?*, *Survivor*, *and Temptation Island*—programs that unabashedly glamorize greed and betrayal by both men and women. While some conscientious public figures try valiantly to shine their spotlights on people who do good, we are still far more fascinated by the tawdrier side of life. The culture of fame and consumption is upon us.

There's also the simple fact that the pace of life is a lot faster than ever before. In this day of "Be all that you can be," "Every person for themselves," and "He who dies with the most toys wins," there's no denying we've lost sight of some of the more noble attributes that used to be held in high regard, such as dignity, discretion, courtesy, humility, and social consciousness. People we hold up as examples today possess these qualities in abundance.

The belief system called myself is not about having the best designer clothes, drinking a wine spritzer instead of what you really want, batting your eyes and playing coy instead of using your brains and wit, taking your boss's shortcomings "lying down," or pretending to be fulfilled by less than enough. Rather, it is a system that sets up choices and experiences for us and thus continually reinforces itself through our habitual ways of acting. Our belief system is our total way of experiencing life, the context or filter through which perceptions are screened. In other words, our belief system helps shape our reality.

> *"To be nobody but yourself in a world which is doing its best, night and day, to make you everybody else means to fight the hardest battle which any human being can fight, and never stop fighting."*
>
> ~e. e. cummings~

Being reconciled to ourselves as we are is a first mark of self-esteem. Whatever we see as our "self" must have a place of dignity in our own hearts and consciousness before we can become individualized as personalities.

Of course, if we take just the tiniest incremental steps in line with what we see as our essential values and goals, we will move healthfully in this direction. However, in order to take these little steps we must pay attention to the way we "speak" to ourselves mentally, sub-vocally. Our habits, actions, vices, and attachments are but a language through which we can more clearly understand the belief system called myself.

Treating Yourself As If You Count

> *"It's a funny thing about life — those who are willing to settle for less than the best usually get it."*
>
> ~W. Somerset Maugham~

We are creatures of habit, so an important action is the habit of treating ourselves as if we count, by doing the things that enhance our dignity, daily intentions, and most cherished values. By treating ourselves as if we count in our own eyes, we break our adherence to a conduct code that discounts and negates who we really are, and what we really enjoy and value.

Treating ourselves well is a step that can rapidly build self-esteem. Research studies show that people who have high self-esteem regularly reward themselves in tangible and intangible ways. Their tangible rewards consist of concrete items they enjoy, for example, purchases, activities, and "time-off" for vacations. Their intangible rewards may be in the form of self-statements that say they have done the best they could, or that they are happy with themselves. More importantly, their rewards carry with them messages, both symbolic and actual, that say they are worthwhile, that they deserve good things, and that they have succeeded in their own eyes. By documenting and celebrating their successes, they ensure that these successes will reoccur.

Another secret behind treating yourself as if you count is learning to accept others as if they count. A good practical habit to start this would be to notice, non-judgmentally, what we say mentally when we believe others are foolish, unkind, or deserving of criticism. When we find ourselves mentally judging others or saying anything unkind or negative to them, we should make a point of reminding ourselves, "They are doing the best they can right now." Once we have stopped judging, we must be able to mentally forgive them, and at the same time forgive ourselves for having been so judgmental and reactive. Forgiving ourselves dissolves unhealthy attitudes, about us and about the other person. We are released from brutal, self-criticizing emotions when we stop criticizing others. In a very real way, there is no one else "out there," and our criticism of others often is nothing more than self-criticism: we cannot accept or tolerate in ourselves what we get angry at in others.

Self-criticism increases our fear and belief that living a blemish-free existence is necessary. The only cure is to help ourselves feel secure within ourselves, so that we eventually come to see that no matter what we do, we will not cast ourselves out of our own hearts. For some, self-acceptance and treating themselves as if they count may be the first experience of approval and security they have had. By reducing our self-criticism, we can reduce resistance to ourselves, decrease distrust, and increase love of self and others. Our own psyche is healed by putting our arms around ourselves, if only figuratively and emotionally, and saying to ourselves within our heart-of-hearts that we are all right as human beings even when we are imperfect, even if we retreat to a place with safety and security.

This is a sure route, although an unusually difficult one for some people, to a consecrated feeling toward the self; it is also a sure path toward enhancing self-esteem since nothing can be gained by negative self-judgments. Putting a stop to our self-defeating actions and habits is a first step and a very helpful practice to aid our growth and self-respect.

Understanding the distinction between self-esteem and personality is also important. Your personality is the complex of characteristics that distinguishes you from everyone else. Self-esteem is having confidence and satisfaction in the complexity of who you are. Self-esteem refers to how well you think of and value yourself, how much you're worth in your own eyes, and the power you allow yourself to have. In other words, you have the capacity to define who you are and then decide if you like the identity or not.

When you evaluate the level of your self-esteem, you look at intrinsic qualities such as whether you believe you're a useful person, how much you trust yourself, and how self-satisfied you feel. Are you pleased or unhappy about what you've accomplished in your life so far? How well do you relate to others? How comfortably do you accept responsibility for your actions? Whether your self-esteem level is high or low depends on how you feel about your sense of value, your accomplishments, your relationships, your abilities, and your sense of responsibility.

Some career workshops survey personality traits by taking into account how others perceive a person. A secretary whose supervisor had undergone an intensive self-awareness seminar designed to give individuals enhanced interpersonal skills and help them grow as persons, was troubled to find that this nationally-known workshop's approach was to send confidential questionnaires to co-workers and friends of participants so as to determine how the individual was seen by others.

"I want to learn how to be stronger as the person I truly am, not learn to be more sensitive to what other people think of me," this woman said. What we need to learn is how to strengthen ourselves from within, not abandon our own perceptions while we pay greater attention to what others think. In this case, the woman wanted more distance and protection from "what others think." Her supervisor, on the other hand, felt he had been insensitive to the opinions of his staff and so wanted their feedback. In this example, the woman knew herself well enough to know what she needed by way of feedback and information.

Another individual, who had a Ph.D., and was an accomplished entrepreneur, recalled that a physician had advised him that he was not "constitutionally equipped" for accomplishing the goals he had in mind.

"He told me, I was 'too weak,' that I would hurt myself physically and die young if I tried to do what I longed to do. He said that my 'sights were set too high for the body and the mind' that I had been born with. While this information concerned me for a short time, I then decided—quite consciously—that I would live my life as I'd intended. If it meant that I would live a shorter life because of my body's limitations, then so be it. What I refused to do was treat myself as an invalid just because I had low energy or some physical weaknesses. All people have something that they can use as an excuse to stop them from living life fully. In the end this doctor's remarks only gave me more determination." As his coach, he thanked me for reminding him to treat himself as if he counted. He is grateful for trusting himself to lead the fulfilling life he has always wanted. His dream is a reality and he is proving to be a medical miracle at the same time.

A loving attitude toward ourselves helps us heal or maintain a healthy self-esteem. Our growth also requires that we step away from the crowd, even if it scares us to do so. When we love ourselves as we are, we give ourselves the strength and confidence to move in our own directions, leave the safety of what has been called "the herd," and grow into who we truly are.

Growing toward the expression of our true way of being requires mastering a number of new skills, such as experimenting with novel behaviors, attitudes, meeting new people, and being in new situations. Brutal force or punitive self-messages in the face of these lessons, during which we tell ourselves we "can't" make it, or that we don't know what to do, are bound to recreate habitual avoidance patterns. These self-statements can only do us harm. How much better it would be if we could accept the part of ourselves we see as hesitant or threatened. Like a kind and stable parent talking to a child, we can also tell ourselves that, step-by-step, little by little, we will learn how to deal with the unknown. How much wiser to accept the part of ourselves we have long felt to be loathsome, and by doing so incorporate the belief that we count into our consciousness of who we are.

Finishing Up:
The Finishing Touches to Express Your Distinctive Self

"THE WORLD WAS MY OYSTER, BUT I USED THE WRONG FORK."
~OSCAR WILDE~

In 1922, Emily Post said, "To make a pleasant and friendly impression is not only good manners, but equally good business." No doubt, she would have eagerly confronted the challenges of today: road rage, air rage, cell phone rage, computer rage. And yes, even Starbucks rage. We live in angry times.

Job insecurity, terrorist attacks, mega-merges, reengineering, and downsizing, along with the technological advances that have us living, working, and communicating in ways we hardly could have imagined just a few years ago, leave us too busy or too stressed to remember common sense must be common practice in organizations and everyday life. Finishing touches equate good manners with good business and common sense, and help to instill the self-confidence that sets you on the road to success. These touches will make a difference in every circumstance to ground people in the timeless fundamentals as they work their way through a fast-changing world.

Happily, finishing touches and etiquette aren't a series of trivial dictates to be tediously memorized. Instead, finishing touches and etiquette is the art of appearing poised and gracious while you make others feel comfortable. The question to constantly ask yourself is "How am I showing up?" Savvy self-promotion demands awareness of and attention to opportunity. People with high self-esteem are very aware of their environment and more important, they use the environment purposefully. They are able to see what is happening. They process what they see in creative ways and they use their environment to their advantage. How you present yourself, in every facet of your life—visually, verbally, and nonverbally—directly affects the impact and influence you have on the perceptions of others.

In today's business world, practical and gracious ways of dealing with people make interactions easier and more comfortable for everyone. In fact, as common courtesy becomes less and less common, the nuances of etiquette are an essential component of career success. Practices that were part of every youngster's home and school training in an earlier generation have often gotten lost as our society has become more fragmented and mobile. Changes in the role of women have further complicated etiquette issues in many situations.

The general manager of a television station recently requested business etiquette coaching for the new staff. "These people have celebrity status in our community," she explained. "They attend prestigious functions where they are highly visible representatives of the station. Frankly, many of them are awkward. They don't know which fork to use or how to make a proper introduction. It's an embarrassment to the station."

In the past, most people at work didn't worry about table manners; sexual harassment; non-sexist, ethnically correct forms of address and language; the special problems of women executives working and traveling in ways unknown to past generations; the new codes concerning romantic involvement at work; politically correct ethics; or diversity. The new manners of the high technology generation: integrating the disabled in the workplace; the relations of men and women working together not only as equals, but in new configurations of gender and age, which changes a lot of ideas about rank and relating, are only some of the revolutionary changes taking place in our lives.

We are all aware that the way in which we dress has the power to arouse us, to reassure us, to shock us. What few of us realize is that we are exercising that power and that every time we put on clothes we are giving signals to others about ourselves, and our own understanding of our place in society. Body packaging reveals to us those messages that we are often unconsciously transmitting.

What is style? For some, it's just an advanced form of fashion, a kind of consistent rightness about clothes that distinguishes the would-be-chic from the real elite. And for others, it's the ultimate expression of character. Defining style has long preoccupied not just those who don't seem to have it, but also those who have been celebrated for it. "Style is about surviving, about having been through a lot and making it look easy," says C. Z. Guest.

Style is a subject of endless allure precisely because it can't be neatly defined. In its mystery lies its power. Resourcefulness, in many cases, the refusal to take a meaningless no for an answer, isn't often thought to be an element of style. But when you know what you want and know how to get it gracefully—that's style.

Elegance, the idea anyway, is always the favor of fashion. Elegance is research. It's knowing what and knowing when. Elegance is being a master of correct behavior. So, let us add originality, verve, and certain fearlessness to our list of vital ingredients for a stylish life. Discipline, elegance, wit, resourcefulness, originality; these are the core qualities possessed by people with high self-esteem who know the value of style and how it can affect their lives.

Most people admire the people who use style to propel them out of anonymity and into the limelight. These people, beyond their expertise and experience, can be considered masters of conversation. We celebrate their rich diversity and marvel at all they pack into their lives. We envy the way they take their talents and refine them to the point that they don't just shine; they glow.

Finally, be increasingly fastidious about your personal grooming. Not being groomed well is unattractive on the young and positively shocking on older people. Some things do not alter with time and technology. When it comes to selling either your personal charms or professional abilities, body language and the proper grooming talk loudest of all.

An assured, confident presence is easy to recognize in others, but harder to identify and assess in ourselves. An assured presence is really an entire set of behaviors and attitudes that say clearly to others, "I am important and so are you." Exactly what behaviors convey that assurance and poise? In the first few moments of an interaction, we telegraph dozens of messages through our posture, facial expressions, eye contact, handshake, introductions, table manners, and gestures. Orchestrate those elements to maximize your impact.

"LONG BEFORE I AM NEAR ENOUGH TO TALK TO YOU ON THE STREET, IN A MEETING, OR AT A PARTY, YOU ANNOUNCE YOUR SEX, AGE, AND CLASS TO ME THROUGH WHAT YOU ARE WEARING, AND VERY POSSIBLY GIVE ME IMPORTANT INFORMATION (OR MISINFORMATION) AS TO YOUR OCCUPATION, ORIGIN, PERSONALITY, OPINIONS, TASTES, SEXUAL DESIRES, AND CURRENT MOOD. BY THE TIME WE MEET AND CONVERSE, WE HAVE ALREADY SPOKEN TO EACH OTHER IN AN OLDER AND MORE UNIVERSAL TONGUE."

~ALLISON LURIE, AUTHOR OF *THE LANGUAGE OF CLOTHES*~

Expressing Your Distinctive Self

By choosing to act in accordance with our own values, we grow in insight and understanding. We also strengthen our muscles of self-respect and self-understanding. With each conscious choice to live out our best, most ethical, most generous self, we become more fully human, with a stronger self-image, self-concept, and self-esteem. With each blind, mechanistic, or programmed-by-other's choice, we negate our rightful human and most genuine personal qualities.

Choosing rightly, and in integrity with what we truly want, we learn about our strengths. We also notice our weaknesses. As we choose what is most helpful to us, we feel our power growing. Every time we consciously choose something, however insignificant it might seem, in line with what we feel is highest and best in ourselves, we support our true-life goals. Also, we reinforce the idea that we are good, valuable, and worthwhile. This reinforces our next proper, healthful choice. Thus, a more positive cycle takes hold of our habits, thinking, and outcomes.

When our actions affirm what we love, we grow. We grow by moving step-by-step, choice-by-choice, in the direction of whatever it is our inner self tells us we need at a given time or in a given situation. Again and again, we must affirm our essential self through our choices. If we can cultivate an 'ear' for the subjective delight, ethic, and preferences of our inner self and move responsibly toward that, we grow whole with a strong self-esteem to serve as our foundation from which to choose.

The shape and spirit of each honorable, truthful act changes us; these transform and express us as we are at our best. We are thus gradually given the will and power to break the bonds of our self-defeating, self-negating habits, fears, and robotic attitudes. In this way all choices, all day-to-day decisions have the energy to transform our lives if we are but open to the messages and cues from our inner, creative power and the way in which this power relates us to outer life, relationships, and work.

No book, seminar, or evangelical expert can choose these directions for us. Nor is there a pill to swallow that will bring about the uplifting effects that healthful choices can have on our lives. Self-honesty, awareness, and an ongoing inward listening can open our hearts to our inner predisposition and talents, and thereby help us with our growth, development, and self-esteem.

By and large, if we continue to choose healthfully, we end up trusting ourselves. Thus, recovering the skill of tuning in to our own inner world transforms the simplest acts so that eventually the outer world more positively mirrors our inner world. In this way, we find an important key to recovering our lost capacities. Even in late adulthood, this recapturing process, this more elegant and concrete expression, is possible. In fact, this course may point to the primary work of adulthood, since the work of childhood has other requirements and lessons.

"What is a weed?
A Plant whose virtues have not yet been discovered."
~Ralph Waldo Emerson~

After all this is said, an approach for expressing your distinctive self for high self-esteem entails these steps:

- That we identify the values, ethics, and behaviors we cherish, toward which we are predisposed and which have a creative power that is generally beyond our intellectual, logical expression.

- That we plan a small, safe, gradual, and perhaps even conservative approach to bringing our essential inclinations into being. In small steps, we choose to demonstrate what we genuinely value.

- That at least part of our energies and attention be focused on the question of how we reward ourselves; that we listen inwardly to locate those actions that are attractive to us and beneficial to us in a long-term, holistic sense; and that we discover which actions, although actually repugnant, we do mechanistically in order to "fit in," gain approval, conform, or defeat ourselves.

- That we learn to tolerate some tension, discomfort, or pain (if that is required) so as to actively "stand in" for ourselves and treat ourselves as if we count in our own eyes. This way we slowly break the vise-like grip our unproductive, habitual response patterns have over us, and we learn how to make meaningful choices, even when these are not easy or "comfortable."

- That we learn the power of style for expressing our distinctive selves. Our first impressions can be effective or they can be disastrous, but they are forever lasting. No matter what you do, the image you portray is your calling card and is vital to how others perceive you. People are sizing you up within the first three to four seconds of an encounter; they're making judgments about you at seven seconds; and within thirty seconds, they've made at least eleven assumptions about you. These assumptions include social status, economic status, education, occupation, marital status, ancestry, trustworthiness, credibility, likelihood to succeed, approachability, and sense of self. Remember that your life is your message, and you are solely responsible for your choices…so learn to choose well.

- That we locate a competent coach, support group, spiritual leader, or counselor if we feel overburdened, blocked, threatened, inordinately guilt-ridden, or isolated when undertaking any of these steps, so as to responsibly attend to the pain, risks, terror, or discomforts inherent in our own growth into full personhood with high self-esteem.

> "WATCH YOUR THOUGHTS, THEY BECOME YOUR WORDS;
> WATCH YOUR WORDS, THEY BECOME YOUR ACTIONS;
> WATCH YOUR ACTIONS, THEY BECOME YOUR HABITS;
> WATCH YOUR HABITS, THEY BECOME YOUR CHARACTER;
> WATCH YOUR CHARACTER, FOR IT BECOMES YOUR DESTINY.
> YOUR LIFE IS YOUR MESSAGE. LEARN TO CHOOSE WELL."
> ~SCHUYLER MORGAN~

Although we may dearly want self-expression, it will elude us unless we are open to the creative power contained within. In the final analysis, nothing less than scrupulous honesty with our self is called for. More than that, the daily acting out of our "highest self" promotes our wholeness. Our own choices and daily actions decree whether we will be able to act out the essential truth and meaning of ourselves for a life enriched by high self-esteem.

A certain detachment is involved at this level of high self-esteem —a detachment that makes one able to be objective to one's self, as well as to the dictates and expectations of society. Only the person who acts and chooses authentically brings vitality, uniqueness, and a spontaneous richness to their activities. Through this energy, for want of a better word, through this essential connectedness to self, the individual serves themselves and others. And, ultimately, it is through services to self and others that we become fully human, fully alive, and truly ourselves.

In every situation that matters, with high self-esteem, we are masters of correct behavior. We may struggle to establish our individuality and, through style, shield what is unpleasant, unattractive, or outright tragic in our lives. There is a lot to be said for that. That is the power of style, the purest essence of expressing your distinctive self. That is the joy of self-esteem.

About
Schuyler Morgan

Schuyler Morgan, Professional Certified Coach (P.C.C.), is the Founder and President of eCultureCoach.com, a combined network of coaches and consultants who offer an array of services to industries worldwide, spanning all aspects of Enterprise Risk, Security Preparedness, and Contingency Planning for Business Continuity and Crisis Management. She is also the Founder and CEO of Finishing Up – A Contemporary Finishing School with Personal Coaching for Professionals, Young Adults, and Teens. For anyone who wants to realize their potential and avoid the pitfalls of the eCulture Age of Paradox, this trailblazing venture identifies and analyzes the emergence of individual eCulture Leadership, manners, and etiquette, while providing a live, roll-up-your-sleeves guide to confidence, enjoyment, civility, and dignity for profiting in the age we live.

She has authored the booklet "The Art of Recognition," with numerous articles appearing in publications in the U.S. and Canada. She is an alumna of Leadership America, and Editor-in-Chief of the International Coach Federation's Organizational Coach eJournal.

Schuyler, a sought after professional speaker, is often seen as a formidable wit and an irresistible combination of iconoclasm and convention. She doesn't give you rules; she gives you perspective. For those who have stumbled through life wondering if there are any easy answers, the happy news is, Schuyler helps you find them.

Schuyler delivers her revolutionary eCulture Leadership coaching to individuals, entrepreneurs, and organizations' top talent. She coaches them to radically shift their thinking and break out of their comfort zones, an absolute requirement for a competitive edge in this turbulent age of paradox. Her alertness to cutting edge issues and trends keeps her coaching sharp and focused.

Time and again, clients find Schuyler to be a leader in self-concept, in attitudes, and in her actions. She has the personal insight and initiative to express her own perspectives on situations that help her clients find their own wisdom regarding the issues they face. She is very aware of her environment and articulate in describing her understanding of it and her vision of how it may be improved.

Schuyler is in a unique position to coach individuals and organizations toward their potential by combining her knowledge of human dynamics and high performance organizational cultures. She seems particularly able to understand people and the human factor in situations, especially in today's demanding fast paced environments. Schuyler has the energy, confidence, and spirit to initiate in all environments, and to influence outcomes, a necessary sign of authentic leadership abilities. These abilities are well developed in her coaching approach. She blends the strength of maturity with the enthusiasm, vigor, and spontaneity of youth.

Schuyler resides in Oakland, California. To contact her, visit www.eCulutureCoach.com or www.FinishingUp.com or call (510) 653-6868.

The Truth About You:
Five Keys to Enhancing Self-Esteem

by Laura Davis

One of the wonderful things about getting older that few people talk about is becoming more "comfortable in your own skin." With life experience, most of us become more aware of our strengths as well as our limitations. By the time we reach a certain age, we've experienced successes and failures. If we've reflected upon and learned from our experiences, we have gained wisdom. We know we can get through challenging times and create joy in our lives regardless of the circumstances.

This has been the truth for me. Personally, I would not want to be an adolescent again. Do you remember what it was like to be a teenager? I remember feeling shy and uncertain. When I was 15, my father was promoted and we moved to a small town in New York State. The move was in the middle of my sophomore year in the midst of a snowy winter. I remember walking into a new classroom with all eyes upon me, checking out and evaluating "the new girl." This experience could be daunting for even the most confident young girl.

As I attempted to acclimate to my new environment, I found I would look around at others to see where I fit in. As a teenager, I would assess myself, my looks, and my accomplishments, then compare myself to others in my class, in women's magazines, and on T.V. Did I measure up? What would it take for me to be happy, for me to be one of the "charmed ones?" Then, as now, societal messages streamed at me to be prettier, to be smarter, to be cuter, and to of course use the product the advertisers were promoting at the time. While "benchmarking" may be useful in business or sports, it's not always helpful in developing character and personality. Although I had the inner wisdom even then to understand that "racket," I was still influenced by it.

At about the same age, I remember coming across a book that first introduced to me a different way of evaluating my worth. The book was a collection of short stories published by <u>American Girl</u> magazine called "Stories to Live By." One of the stories was about a popular young girl who hung out with the right kids, had a good-looking and athletic boyfriend, and wore the most beautiful, stylish clothes. And yet, she was as miserable as any teenage girl could be.

As the story unfolded, she began to be true to herself. She realized that she didn't like the other "cool" kids who were often cruel and shallow to those who didn't fit in, nor did she really care for her boyfriend. Instead, she preferred the "nerdier" guy who listened to her dreams and interests and who remembered to ask about what was important to her. She also preferred reading and studying things that weren't "cool," rather than going to parties and being what everyone expected her to be. Gradually, she found the courage to use her own guidance as her compass and to be authentic in the face of risking ridicule and having to forge new friendships.

The story had a powerful impact on the life path I have chosen. As a coach, a large part of my relationship with a client is to guide them in being authentic in their life. We access their own wisdom in discerning what is right for them and what is not. Looking to others for approval is always a losing proposition. So is trying to be something you're not. When Picasso was asked if he considered Van Gogh his favorite painter because he was the best, he replied, "No. Because he is Van Gogh. He is not always good, but he is always Van Gogh." And so it is with each of us. We can be our best in terms of ourselves only.

Many people have lost touch with their inner wisdom and their own true values. What we need to remember is that within each of us is all of the wisdom we'll ever need to solve any kind of problem we may be experiencing. Robert Browning in *Paracelsus* elegantly said, "Truth is within ourselves; it takes no rise from outward things, whate'er you may believe…and, to know, rather consists in opening out a way whence the imprisoned splendour may escape, than in effecting entry for a light supposed to be without."

Reconnecting with this light takes courage. Having someone else tell you what you should be and what you should do seems easier than it is to discover it for yourself. Meanwhile, it takes a lot of unlearning to be all of who we really are.

Many clients who come for coaching have some potential in their lives that they feel they are not currently expressing. There is a gap between where they are and where they want to be. In truth, there is perfection in where they are. More often, it's a question of removing what's in the way of them expressing their greatness. They must first be able to conceive of the possibility of a different way of being.

How does one begin to recognize all of who they are to create a truly fulfilling life? I'm going to outline five essential keys that will get you started on this journey to authentic wholeness. These are the keys to self-esteem on a fundamental, character level:

- separate your worth from externals
- change self-limiting thoughts and self-talk
- use your emotions to identify limited thinking
- examine your beliefs and mental models
- imagine yourself as you want to be

Separate Your Worth from Externals

There is a concept in psychology called "The Social Mirror." The concept is a metaphor for the way we see ourselves based upon the perceptions, opinions, and paradigms that others reflect back to us through their words and behavior. We form images and judgements of ourselves (for example, "I'm not a creative person" or "I'm not good at math") based upon how others see us. Because others may not be seeing us clearly, or are projecting their own weaknesses onto us, and because by definition, the social mirror is a reflection of our past behavior, it is often inaccurate and limiting. In actuality, our world mirrors back to us our beliefs about ourselves. If we can learn to own our core strengths, believe in our capabilities, and have a strong vision of who we are, we can change how others see and treat us. When we do this, the process becomes a positive, rather than a negative feedback loop.

Rather than relying on the views of others or the social mirror as the reflection of your worth, separate your worth from anything external to yourself. Externals can take different forms in our culture. In addition to the self-image we adopt based upon other peoples' perspectives, our Western culture often ties our worth to what we do or achieve, how much money or what kind of possessions we have, and even to the circumstances and events that occur in our lives. Things such as money, looks, performance, and achievements may increase our *social* worth, but each of us has *inherent* worth that is infinite and unchanging.

If our worth is tied to or depends upon anything external to us, then our self-esteem rises and falls along with those externals. That is a very conditional way to live. Instead, I suggest shifting to the recognition that your essential, spiritual self or who you really are at your core is fundamentally right and whole. Being proud of our unique strengths and talents and taking pleasure in expressing them is perfectly appropriate.

While a talent expressed is a way to experience our worth, not expressing a talent doesn't mean that we are any less worthy. Likewise, it's wonderful to feel loved by others and it's a wonderful way to feel our worthiness. But if no one loves us at this moment, we are in no way less of a person. When we forget what powerful, spiritual beings we all are naturally, we use externals to fill a sense of lack. We all know people who are constantly seeking approval, control, or security or who have become cynical because they have forgotten who they really are.

What can we do to recognize and affirm our self-worth and have a healthy self-concept or high self-esteem independent of these external factors? First, learn to separate your behavior and your uncomfortable feelings from who you really are. In English we say, "I am angry," while other languages express angry emotions by saying the equivalent of "I have anger." This is an important distinction. If who you really are is not your emotions or your behavior, and your feelings and actions are things that you experience, then you are free to change feelings and behavior without threatening your identity.

For example, let's say that a wonderful job that you wanted and didn't get was offered to someone else. If you can see that not getting the job may have been the result of not having the appropriate skills, experience, or training, then you are appropriately separating the situation from your value as an individual. However, if you tell yourself that you're a person who never gets what she or he wants or that somehow you're just not good enough, then you are limiting yourself and your choices unnecessarily. This is a self-destructive choice of thoughts that can lead to lowered self-esteem.

Change Self-Limiting Thoughts and Self-Talk

What we say when we talk to ourselves is an important thing to become conscious of throughout the day. All of us have conversations going on in our heads literally all of the time. Our self-talk can be in spoken words or in unspoken thoughts. Self-talk can take the form of feelings, impressions, and even physical cues such as a "gut feeling" or a racing heartbeat. Most of our self-talk is so habitual we aren't even aware of it. At times, our self-talk comes in feelings that can't quite be put into words. However, it is a different voice than the voice of our intuition. I've noticed my own self-talk can be like white noise or chatter. The voice of my intuition is more still and calm. True intuition is always helpful and accurate, while self-talk may or may not be.

Regardless of the form our self-talk or internal conversation takes, it is a reflection of our perceptions and beliefs. Perceptions are the ways in which we see things, based on how we think they "should" be. Likewise, we think things "should" be a certain way based upon our beliefs and values. In effect, our beliefs act as filters or lenses on the world. If we have on rose-colored glasses, everything looks pink. If our lenses are blue, well, everything looks blue to us.

In common language, other words we might use to describe perceptions include attitudes, perspectives, opinions, points of view, etc. Whatever we call them, they influence how we interpret an event or situation in our life. So, when something happens or someone says something to us, it does not *cause* our reaction. Our response is up to us. However, the event or person triggers an interpretation of what happened based upon our perceptions. Our perceptions then influence our self-talk or the story we tell ourselves about what happened.

Depending on the nature of the story we tell ourselves, we are going to have an emotional or feeling response. This feeling may be good or bad, positive or negative. How we feel about it then influences our behavior. For example, I used to feel nervous and uncomfortable when speaking in front of a group. I'm sure this is a feeling a few of us can relate to. When I felt nervous, the self-talk that was often going on in my head was that I am not making sense and that everyone will know I don't know what I'm talking about.

Obviously, holding that belief about me, and feeling the feeling those thoughts produced affected my behavior and performance. When I was telling myself that no one was going to understand me, I'm sure I wasn't expressing myself very clearly. I've since learned to change my self-talk by focusing on my audience and not on my self-consciousness. If I hadn't recognized my negative self-talk and done something to change it, I probably would have stopped speaking in front of groups. I wouldn't have gained the experience and practice to become a better speaker.

The good news is, once we become aware of our own self-limiting thoughts and self-talk, we can redirect the outcome of this cycle at any point in the process. One simple quick coaching tip is to learn the Stop/Challenge/Focus technique. This technique is adapted from Larry Wilson, the founder of The Wilson Learning Corporation and Pecos River Learning Centers. Here is how it works. As you catch yourself about to habitually react to a situation negatively, just stop, and take a deep breath. You catch yourself in the moment, and mentally interrupt your own internal dialogue. In neuro-linguistic programming terms, you create a pattern interrupt by breaking the flow and direction of the negative energy.

Next, ask yourself, "If I act on this negative self-talk, what is likely to happen?" Keep asking: "What am I telling myself about this situation and how is that making me feel? Is there a better way to look at this situation? How can I reach for a better feeling or thought about it?" Often, a situation is not as bad as it seems initially, but we "awfulize" it and exaggerate its dire consequences to ourselves and to others.

Instead, we can redirect or pivot from our original line of thinking and redirect our focus. Which brings us to the last part of the Stop/Challenge/Focus technique: focusing on what you now want. You can facilitate this focus by asking yourself the following questions: "What do I want to happen? What do I want my behavior to be? What do I need to tell myself so that I can achieve it?"

Once the focus of our attention has shifted to what we want, we are then in the position of bringing it into physical reality. Now we can focus on reprogramming our minds with more empowering beliefs and self-concepts that directly impact our ability to be successful and fulfilled in life. There are many techniques and resources that can assist you in this reprogramming, such as the Silva method, creative visualization, neuro-linguistic programming, spiritual mind treatment, affirmations, the Sedona Method, and countless others. A coach can help you decide what's best for you given your current beliefs and personal preferences.

Use Your Emotions to Identify Limited Thinking

Being aware of our self-limiting thoughts and self-talk does not mean that we must be constantly worried about the thoughts we think. We don't want to be ever vigilant about never thinking a negative thought. Since it would be almost impossible to monitor all of the thoughts and impressions that occur to us in any given day, it is fortunate that we come equipped with another tool to help us discern the quality of our self-talk. That tool is our awareness of negative emotion. The problem is, most of us are so used to feeling a little bit overwhelmed or a little bit unhappy or a little bit depressed that we may have forgotten what it feels like to feel good.

The good news is we can train ourselves to become more aware of what we are feeling. This is vitally important. A less-than-positive emotion is an alarm or signal to alert us that we're focusing on a limiting belief about ourselves and our ability to handle a particular circumstance or situation. The signal is useful in letting us know that we're coming from a fearful and not an empowered position.

When we touch a hot stove it hurts and we pull our hand away quickly. The pain alerts us that touching the hot stove is harmful to our welfare so we stop doing it. In the same vein, our negative emotions alert us that we're focusing on a limiting thought about ourselves or our lives that is impeding our ability to be effective. Since we can't stop thinking a thought, when we catch ourselves focused on a negative thought, we must replace it with a more positive one. We must focus on our vision and on what we desire to create out of the situation.

One story that really drives this point home is that of the Great Wallenda. The Wallenda family was renowned for their spectacular circus act comprised of acrobatics and tightrope walking. In particular, Karl Wallenda, the patriarch of the family, performed many death-defying tightrope feats walking high above the ground between tall buildings and even over Niagara Falls without a net.

He eventually fell to his death in his 70's while tightrope walking between two tall buildings in Puerto Rico. Since he had been so successful in the past in even more threatening situations, people wondered why he died when he did and under those circumstances. When asked "why now?" his widow replied, "All of his life Karl focused on success and on getting to the other side. He knew he could do it. But in the last year of his life, he started to focus on 'not falling.' He started to wonder if he could fail."

This story illustrates that the power of our attention and awareness is not to be underestimated. If our circumstances are not as we would like them to be, we can use the situations we find ourselves in to discover our beliefs. Once we know what our beliefs are, we can change them so that our results are in accordance with our desires.

Examine Your Beliefs and Mental Models

Everything depends upon your attitude about yourself. And your attitude about yourself comes from the beliefs you've accepted are the truth about you. Henry Ford said, "Whether you think you can or think you can't—you are right." A dramatic example of how we often mentally accept unreal limitations can be found in how elephants are trained for the circus.

A baby elephant is first chained to a post with a heavy metal chain. If the baby elephant tries to go beyond a certain point, the chain painfully binds its leg and keeps it from moving further. Soon, the baby elephant doesn't venture as far and the trainer replaces the chain with a strong rope. If the elephant attempts to go beyond the predetermined point, again it is restrained since the rope will painfully chafe its leg. Before long, the baby elephant has grown into an adult and can be held in check within the area by a thin string around its leg. The elephant has been conditioned to believe that it will be hurt if it ventures outside of its comfort zone. Certainly, this is a false belief, as a fully-grown elephant can easily break a thin string to be able to move fully and to be free.

While you might say, "that's just for elephants," how often do we accept false beliefs about ourselves because of our experience with some circumstance or event? While it may seem as though the circumstances or events we find ourselves in are limiting us, it is really our beliefs about the circumstances that matter. To take it a step further, while it may seem as though the circumstances and events that occur in your life are a result of some outer cause, all that you experience is a result of your state of consciousness. Completely accepting the idea that your beliefs form your experiences is necessary. Blaming others or circumstances and events might be easier in the short run, but then you remain a victim of these things forever. Accepting personal responsibility for changing your beliefs gives you hope and power.

So, where do we begin if we have a desire to create different results in our lives? First, we need to recognize our beliefs so that we can choose to keep or to change them. If we don't know what they are, it's difficult to work with them. So, awareness of the beliefs that serve us and awareness of the beliefs that limit us is the first step. Fortunately, our beliefs are not deeply buried in our subconscious awaiting excavation. They are just habits of thought (thoughts we keep thinking). But because they are so habitual, they may go undetected.

For example, in working with a coaching client about issues of abundance and financial health, I posed the question, "What's getting in the way of your achieving abundant financial success?" She immediately, replied, "I'm afraid that all of my friends will be jealous of me." I replied, "That's an interesting belief." She looked at me as though I'd awakened her to a whole new reality. She exclaimed, "My goodness you're right! It never occurred to me that my fear is just a belief and that I can change it, and therefore my reality if I want to!"

There are many tools and techniques available to change beliefs, as I mentioned earlier when referencing changing self-limiting thoughts and self-talk. What you're doing is changing your belief systems and increasing your level of understanding. You are looking at the situation from a "higher" point of view. Ultimately, the process can be as simple as discarding those beliefs that are not bringing you the results you want and replacing them with new ones.

One simple technique is to "act as if" the new belief, and therefore the desired result, is already true for you. For most of us, it just doesn't seem logical to accept on faith that simply imagining successful results can actually move you toward them. We're often too impatient to wait for the cumulative results of "acting-as-if" to take effect. Some people give up immediately because they analyze too much and try to figure out how it works. That's why it's helpful to suspend disbelief for awhile and to just experiment. Building a new self-image generally doesn't happen overnight, but rather is a cumulative process. Trust that in time, your new reality will catch up to your desire.

In effect, you build bridges between your old and new beliefs as your reality shifts around you. In the meantime, you will often be in the situation of telling yourself that something is true although physical data contradicts it. For example, you may say, "I am abundant and never want for anything," while your desk is piled high with unpaid bills. You must realize that you are the one who produced the physical evidence of lack that still faces you through your beliefs. The good news is that as you alter that belief about yourself, the physical evidence will gradually begin to "prove" your new belief as faithfully as it did your old one.

Imagine Yourself As You Want to Be

In his classic work *Psycho-Cybernetics*, Maxwell Maltz said, "Creative imagination is not something reserved for the poets, the philosophers, or the inventors. For imagination sets the goal or 'picture' that our automatic mechanism works on. We act, or fail to act, not because of 'will' as is so commonly believed, but because of imagination." In fact, I'm sure many of us can attest to the ineffectiveness of using willpower to change our behaviors and self-image to improve our self-esteem. The list of unfulfilled New Year's resolutions is frustratingly long for most of us. Yet, there is another way to change our beliefs, and therefore our feelings and behaviors. The way is through creative visualization and imagination.

Fortunately, our brain doesn't know or care whether what we think about is real or imaginary. Test this for yourself by vividly imagining yourself biting into a sour lemon. You are likely to be salivating and puckering your lips in response to this imaginary fruit just as you would if you were really eating it. Since we've already established that what we focus on and think about becomes true for us, we can create a new mental image of how we'd like things to be and have it take shape in physical reality.

The classic research on this was done with basketball players attempting to make free throw shots. The researchers formed three groups of players with very equal skills and capabilities for this experiment. A control group changed nothing over a 21-day period. The second group practiced shooting free throws in the gym for 21 days. The third group never touched a basketball and yet visualized themselves making the free throws successfully in the theater of their imaginations. Remarkably, the latter two groups each improved by about 24 percent, while the control group stayed the same. Later they found that the visualizers' success could be further increased if they engaged all of their senses and focused on seeing the ball swoosh through the hoop, heard the sound the ball makes when it goes in, felt the emotions of pride and success when they made the shot, and so on.

How can this be so and why is it important to visualize success in terms of images and feelings instead of just willpower or determination? And how does this relate to self-esteem or self-image? The word image forms the root of the word imagination. When you use your imagination, the part of the brain that is engaged is your right brain. Most of us have heard generalizations about split-brain research that can be useful in understanding how this works at a high level. The right brain allows us to think holistically, spatially, and imaginatively while the left brain is logical, sequential, and analytical. To become whole and fully functioning, we want to integrate both right and left-brain functioning to be all of who we are. However, our culture and training largely favors left-brain functioning.

Yet, if we try to change our self-image solely through the verbal, logical, left side of the brain, it's not going to work very well. That's not the left brain's job. While no part of the brain has ever been identified with "the mind" and consciousness is certainly not limited to the brain's functioning alone, there is a correlation between the right brain and the spiritual creative experience that is so hard to put into words.

Another way to explain this is to think about the left brain as generally working with the conscious mind, while the right brain tends to work with the subconscious mind. So, since the way you think and act is intimately bound to your self-image, you're not going to change your self-image and improve your self-esteem by working with the part of your brain that deals in words alone—your left brain. This is an error that many people make in attempting to change beliefs. They might utter the right words, but the image is not fully developed in the person's imagination.

The way to form a bridge between your old beliefs and your new physical reality is to use your imagination to form a mental picture or image of the desired physical result. Aristotle said, "The soul never thinks without a picture." Einstein said, "Imagination is more important than knowledge." The writer Emmet Fox also wrote about the importance of vision and imagination with the concept of "the mental equivalent." The phrase "the mental equivalent" refers to the fact that everything that exists in the material world is just the concrete expression of a mental equivalent that you hold in consciousness. In other words, everything is created in mind first as an idea.

Think about it this way. Before building a home, an architect starts with a blueprint. Before painting a picture, the artist has an idea of the image and the feeling state he or she wants to create for the person looking at it. In the same way, a mental blueprint and image is where we need to start if we are going to have a bigger idea of who we are and can be. The most effective way to do this is to consistently use your imagination to visualize and picture you as you'd like to be. Even more important, you must find the feeling place or emotional equivalent and think and feel from the desired state as if it already is "true" in physical reality. Since whatever enters your life and therefore affects your belief in yourself is just the material expression of some belief in your own mind, the key to a better you and a better life, as Emmet Fox said, is to "Change your mind and keep it changed."

So, how do we do this? Let's say you are a salesperson and your goal is to make a sale to a particular client. You can spend just 15 to 20 minutes a day rehearsing this success in your mind in order to develop a mental equivalent. However, the mental equivalent is not just seeing yourself outside of yourself succeeding at your goal. Instead, you want to get to the underlying desire that you feel this goal would bring to you and feel that as if it is already so. For instance, making the sale might lead to a greater sense of security and a sense of satisfaction in pleasing your client or customer, etc. You want to identify the essence of the feeling state you think achieving this goal would bring to you and imagine it as being so now. You engage all of your senses and experience it fully as if it were really happening. So in this example, you might see your client smiling broadly, saying how pleased they are, feel them excitedly shaking your hand, smell the congratulatory flowers your colleagues have sent you once you get back to the office, and so on.

The metaphysical teacher Neville Goddard expressed this idea beautifully by saying that the key to changing your self-image is to "assume the feeling of the wish fulfilled." That is the secret to forming a true mental equivalent that takes shape in physical reality. While that may sound unscientific to some, modern physics is discovering what the ancient mystics have known for eons: that thoughts are things and the thoughts that we think most often set up vibrational frequencies that attract circumstances and events of similar frequency to us. In other words, our thoughts are a form of magnetic energy and what we think and feel sets up a force field of sorts that attracts to us like situations and experiences. It's a similar principle to how a tuning fork works. If you strike a tuning fork calibrated to high C in a room filled with tuning forks calibrated to various pitches, only the ones calibrated to the same frequency as the high C you struck will sound. This is true regardless of how far away the forks are from one another.

The same principle is at work when we notice how people seem to have recurrent problems. The person with money problems always has money problems. The person with relationship problems always has relationship problems. As we already established, beliefs, conscious or not, are creating these circumstances and conditions. And using our imagination to create a vision of who we want to be can create miraculous events.

To recap, you engage your right brain, which is in tune with the spiritual realm, by using your imagination to:

1) see yourself as you want to be as if it is happening now,

2) engage all of your senses fully,

3) get underneath your desire and conjure up the feeling place of what your desired outcome would bring to you, and

4) release your need to figure out the details of how and when it will come. Allow it to take shape and get out of the way.

To increase our self-esteem and to live a more fulfilling life, it really is as simple as recognizing the truth about ourselves and our self-imposed limitations. Neville summed it up by saying, "To reach a higher level of being, you must assume a higher concept of yourself. If you will not imagine yourself as other than you are, then you remain as you are."

You've now been introduced to some of the keys to begin this journey for yourself. Separating your worth from the world of externals and becoming aware of your self-limiting thoughts and self-talk is the beginning. Once you are aware, use your emotions as signals to alert you to discover and to examine your beliefs. If your beliefs are creating the results you want, give yourself the credit! If you'd like to change the results you are getting, you can change your beliefs to be in alignment with your desires. Finally, using some of the tools and techniques I've outlined briefly here, use your imagination to create a vision of who you want to be.

Just like the young girl in "Stories to Live By," I'm learning to value myself regardless of how I "stack up" to others. Sometimes, I do still compare myself to others, but these days, it happens less and less. I certainly am not free of self-limiting thoughts and self-talk, but now I catch myself in the act and do my best to Stop/ Challenge/Focus.

Now I just do my best to tune into how I'm feeling throughout the day. If I'm feeling anything less than good, I'm focused on a negative thought that has probably become a habit of thought, which is all a belief really is. So, if that belief isn't working in my favor and getting me the results I want, I have the power to change it. That's my cue to refocus on what I want and to imagine myself as I want to be. Acting "as if" it already is does wonders for my self-image.

There is so much more to who we are than the self-image or concept we hold in our conscious minds based upon our past experiences. We are truly multidimensional, powerful beings who are always connected to an infinite source of wisdom and inspiration. Remembering this allows us to recognize our true potential, which is not limited to what's been possible for us until now. I wish you joy on your journey of discovery of the truth about you.

About
Laura Davis

Laura A. Davis & Associates, Inc. is a leadership training and coaching firm that assists individuals and organizations in growing through change by developing people and organizational capabilities. Prior to becoming an executive coach and facilitator, Laura held both line and staff marketing management positions for Exxon, Equifax, and United Parcel Service. The breadth of her experience includes new product development, marketing research, product management, and sales training. After a successful marketing management career, she started her own leadership training and coaching practice.

In addition to her solid business experience, she possesses a unique talent for seeing "the big picture" and for simplifying complex problems to their essential elements. She has designed and delivered workshops focused on culture change through the development of facilitative leadership and coaching skills for managers. She has also facilitated numerous transformational change intitiatives through "soft skills" training and follow-up coaching. Laura's primary areas of expertise include leadership development, team effectiveness, change management, interpersonal communication skills, and personal and organizational transformation. Her focus is on the development of transformational leadership and team skills using accelerated learning techniques to foster open communication, trust, teamwork, innovation, and creativity. Accelerated Learning focuses on mental models or individual belief systems and how they affect individual and organizational success.

Clients learn to create and sustain supportive relationships, systems for continuous learning and change, and methods for tapping into their personal passions to bring energy and focus into their lives and work. Clients learn how to bring all of who they are into their daily activities to achieve greater balance, joy, creativity, and fulfillment in all areas of life. These aspirations and goals are accomplished through interactive and experiential skills training and individual and team coaching.

Laura is a Master Certified Coach (M.C.C.) through the International Coach Federation. She is affiliated with The Forum Corporation/FT Knowledge as a Senior Facilitator and Executive Coach, as well as several other highly regarded firms that offer assessments, training, coaching, and consulting services. She has a B.A. degree in Sociology with Honors from the University of Delaware. She earned her Masters in Business Administration from Emory University on scholarship. She has been an Adjunct Professor in the Business Studies Program at Mercer University in Douglasville, Georgia. Laura has also received recognition as a "Who's Who in America" conferee.

Laura has conducted numerous training seminars and workshops with multicultural audiences at all levels of an organization throughout the country. She has also trained audiences in Korea and Japa for one of the largest global hotel management companies in the world. She has been a speaker at professional coaching conferences and professional associations throughout the U.S. Her partial client list with client quotes is accessible on her website.

Laura is a certified facilitator and distributor of Inscape Publishing Company's (formerly Carlson Learning Company) learning resources. Instrumented learning profiles and the seminars designed around them are powerful learning tools. These programs allow people to simplify complex issues and help them to discover and capitalize on their strengths, to value their differences, and to collaborate successfully.

Likewise, Laura A. Davis & Associates, Inc. utilizes a variety of other validated assessments and learning tools to help individuals understand themselves and others in greater depth in order to appreciate and build upon their uniqueness. These include *Personal Profile System, The Myers-Briggs Type Indicator Assessment, 360 Degree Assessments including Insight 20/20, The Highlands Ability Battery (THAB), The Managerial Assessment of Proficiency and EXCEL Training Program, TotalView Assessment, DecideX, MindMaps, DISCOVERY by PMI Shares, Inc., and Change Management Toolkit.*

For more information on any of these assessments and learning tools, or to contact Laura, send an email to coachlad@bellsouth.net, call her at (404) 327-6330, or visit her website at www.lauraadavis.com.

Authenticity as an Avenue to Living an Awesome Life

by Jordana Tiger

Authenticity became a focus of my practice years ago after finding that many clients were having difficulty achieving success and a level of personal comfort because they were not truly being themselves. They put on facades and tried to please people in order not to hurt or make them angry, and simply because they wanted to fit in and belong. They gave up liking themselves, as well as the opportunity to feel worth and value. To truly honor yourself, you must have the courage to stand up for your beliefs and feelings in the face of the possibility of disappointing others or not being liked. Being you in every moment is true authenticity. Life is so much easier when you base your decisions on your own ethics, values, thoughts, and feelings. You get to live an awesome life full of freedom and self-esteem.

In working with clients, I've found that there are three components to achieve the authenticity that will help you live an awesome life:

- self-acceptance
- lack of worry about what other people think of you
- a level of personal integrity

These components will be the common denominator in the client examples to come.

Self-Acceptance

My car license plate is XCEPTNC. Acceptance. Self-acceptance is one of the key factors in having and maintaining a healthy level of self-esteem. For me, looking at my license plate as I head out for the day has proven to be my best daily affirmation.

Being appreciated, loved, and accepted are crucial parts of human nature. We all want those aspects in our life. Yet, often people give up their true core values and what they believe in to be liked. Unfortunately, they are not being themselves. You always have the choice to honor your own values, yet if you do not accept yourself, it is extremely challenging to tell someone else who you really are. When you accept yourself, and feel good about who you are, you are free to show yourself to others, revealing your authentic self.

John, a 28-year-old attorney, had the type of family that didn't give him much nurturing. As a child, he was left at home often while his parents worked. John was very quiet and shy. He realized in his twenties that he was attracted to men. This was very difficult for him to accept for many reasons. The main reason was that he wanted others to like him. He knew that being gay was going to be a difficult choice, yet he knew that was who he was inside and he wanted to honor that part of himself.

In working with John, it was evident that not being himself was slowly eating away at his self-esteem. He was feeling very unhappy, did not take good care of himself, and was starting to sabotage his career and work relationships. John kept telling me he hated the fact that he felt he had to compromise his beliefs in order to be liked. In time, he was able to see that it was his choice to compromise. He didn't really need to change or hide his sexual orientation. In getting in touch with "choice" as a concept, he was able to see that there were options. He could choose to hide who he was and give up part of his self-esteem, or he could choose to be authentic and honor himself. He finally realized that what was important was that he liked and accepted himself. Therefore, in choosing to celebrate himself in the face of having people not like him, he decided he wanted to come out to his family and friends.

In our work together, John made a list of qualities he liked about himself and he read them aloud each day in the morning and evenings. These positive affirmations helped him get in touch with all of the many things he did like about himself and he eventually took on a higher level of self-esteem as he truly started to believe his statements. He also made a list of all the possible choices he had in handling his sexual "coming out." Through that exercise, he was able to see there were several options. Before, he was stuck in the either/or, black and white thinking that many people adopt. With his self-acceptance and his understanding of choice, he had the ability and perspective to choose which options he wanted to incorporate in his life.

We also worked on role-playing during the sessions so he would feel more comfortable with his coming out conversations. Self-esteem is built upon people believing they are worthy and that their thoughts and feelings are valued and accepted. John started to have a level of self-acceptance that began to improve his self-esteem. He started to believe he was a worthy and valuable individual. John ended up coming out to his family and friends and due to his own positive self-image, they were very accepting. He gradually became his true authentic self and is able to live feeling free.

Thomas, a 56-year-old married man, was up for a huge promotion at his firm. He had worked for years climbing up the ladder of success, yet felt bored with his job. He really did not want the promotion, although he didn't know how to tell his wife. On the side, Thomas had been working as a freelance photographer, a hobby he has had since his youth. His upcoming challenge was going to be deciding whether to take the promotion, or to turn it down so he could finally pursue the career of his dreams. He had not truly accepted himself for wanting to leave a successful career and giving up all the money to pursue a chance at a lifelong dream of being a photographer. He felt he was doing something wrong.

In working with Thomas, I felt that looking at his values and dreams would be very crucial and worth spending time on. Values are who we are at the very core of our being. They tell us what is important. They are not something we do or have. They are who we are. Our values help us stay true to ourselves. When people make decisions based on what is important, there is more happiness and less disappointment. Only when we can stay true to our heart and soul, can we live a fulfilling life.

If you don't know what is important to you, how can you set meaningful goals? There are too many individuals who are stuck in the rut of their career simply because they have trouble accepting their own passions. In working with clients, one of my first tasks for them is to create a list of values. Seeing how many people are involved in their work and personal relationships for the wrong reasons is amazing to me. To realize that you are not really where you want to be is a huge challenge. And making a change is a courageous, sometimes radical act.

Once Thomas got in touch with the depth, meaning, and purpose behind his photography, he began to accept that it was a wise choice to turn down the promotion in order to pursue his true happiness. He came to a place of self-acceptance. He was able to distinguish the difference between making a lot of money versus diving in to his passion. Thomas had made an extremely courageous move in the face of honoring himself, being authentic with who he was inside, and having the personal integrity to match his feelings with what he was about to do. This greatly improved his self-esteem and he felt more confident in telling his wife the truth about his choice. After working with her on her own values, she eventually was supportive of him once she realized that living one's true values is imperative in living an awesome life. They both were able to share in having authenticity as part of the world they created together.

Don't Worry About What Others Think Of You

Many times people do not speak up for themselves because they are too worried about what someone else is thinking. If you give away that energy, you are then living your life for someone else. How is this going to serve you? If you are too attached to the opinions of others, you end up living their life, not yours. You risk losing your authentic self. Learning to "be" and "do" as you please so you have control over your own life is important. There is a saying I learned years ago that has personally helped me to take on this attitude: "What other people think of me is none of my business." This took some time for me to understand and put to use, but think about how powerful that statement really is. Isn't it okay for someone to have his or her own opinion of me? Why should I allow that to change my opinion of myself? People do have a right to their thoughts. If I allow another person's opinion to influence my thoughts, feelings, and actions, whose life am I really living?

Tracy, 39 and single, was interested in creating more depth and intimacy in her friendships. She indicated to me that she wanted a healthy, authentic relationship with others, yet the problem was that she didn't have one with herself first. The few things she knew about herself were things that she said she hid from others because she was worried about what they would think of her. After all, in her family, the only way to be accepted was to do things their way.

Tracy was invited by one of her friends to see a horror movie. She agreed to go. However, after seeing the movie, Tracy told me that she didn't have a good time because the truth is she was terrified the whole time and had nightmares for weeks. She is the romantic comedy type of moviegoer. Tracy told me that she didn't feel good about herself because she felt like once again she didn't speak up for herself. Tracy gave me many examples where she said her self-esteem suffered due to the fact she just couldn't say what was true for her. She was too worried about what others thought. She let herself down, did not keep her word with herself, and her self-esteem continued to deteriorate. She told me she was extremely tired of compromising herself just to get people to like her.

In our work together, I encouraged Tracy to tell someone something about herself at least once a day that she had previously been hesitant to say. Tracy was slowly able to let others know what she really wanted and how she felt. She started feeling more confident in general.

Tracy was also faced with another situation she didn't know how to handle. She was seeing a married man and wanted to stop, yet didn't want him not to like her. Tracy thought about her values, about what is important to her, and I suggested she make her decision based on her own values, thoughts, and feelings. This way she could feel good about the decision because it was solely based on what she felt was important in life.

Over time, we worked on positive affirmations and setting appropriate boundaries so Tracy would start feeling as if she was in control of her own life. She gave up worrying about what others thought when she realized she felt better when she honored her own values. She felt very empowered. She got to see that people liked her better when she was honest about her likes and dislikes; therefore, more respect and a deeper intimacy was created in all her relationships.

Maintain a Level of Personal Integrity

There is no way to lose with integrity; it is always the correct path. Having integrity within yourself allows you to have integrity with all of the parts of your world. Say "yes" when you mean yes, say "no" when you mean no; match your words to your behavior; do what you say you are going to do. This doesn't mean just with other people. Having integrity has a lot to do with keeping your word to yourself.

Diane works in a corporate setting. She has three children and not much free time for herself. However, going to the gym to work out is very important to her. Diane feels very angry and disappointed in herself because she keeps telling herself she will go to the gym four days a week. However, she doesn't make it there at all. Diane is not keeping her word to herself; she is out of integrity with what she says she will do for herself. In making promises to herself that she doesn't keep, her self-esteem has taken a plunge.

Sharon, a good friend of mine, told me about the time she decided to run a marathon. She said to herself that no matter how tired she felt during the run, that she was committed to finishing the race. Halfway through the marathon, she was extremely exhausted. She definitely wanted to stop, but since she told herself she would finish, she kept going. She wanted to keep her word to herself. This really accented her positive self-esteem. She told me while she was running she kept thinking, "Why should I finish?" The answer kept coming, "Because I said I would." Keeping your word to yourself is just a good idea. It is one of the highlights of having terrific self-esteem.

Tara, a 32-year-old office manager, came to me for coaching when she noticed that she had difficulty with friendships. Through the initial interview, she told me the following story. She had plans to go to coffee after work with a co-worker. At the last minute, her best friend invited her to an event that was very important to her. There was no way Tara would be able to go to both events since they were at the same time. Tara decided to lie to her co-worker and say she was sick. Tara went to the event with her best friend, yet felt uncomfortable about it all night. She really liked her co-worker and they had been planning their coffee date for some time. Tara felt she was out of integrity because she didn't honor her previous commitment. She also ended up running into her co-worker that afternoon while she was with her best friend and felt awful. Her stomach was in knots because she had lied, and she was fearful of going back to work the next day having to face her co-worker.

She asked me how she should have handled the situation so she could be in "integrity." I gave her a few suggestions. One, she could have told her best friend that she was happy she was invited to go to the event, but that she had previous plans and felt it was important to honor them. Her best friend probably would have respected her for keeping her commitment, and Tara would have felt great about it as well. If it was extremely important she attend the second event, she could have told her co-worker that she was very happy they had plans and valued their friendship, yet explain to her how important the event was and that she would have to change her plans and reschedule. The issue is honesty. If she were to look at what was important to her, and then take an honest approach with her friends, she could then feel good about herself. She would therefore be honoring herself and others at the same time.

Being in "integrity" gives you a very empowering feeling. When you take a stand for yourself and live your values, you are in complete integrity with yourself. Again, you have the choice to honor your word or not. What kind of character do you want to portray?

If you are happy with your character and traits, you will have an amazing sense of self-esteem, worth, and pride. If you keep your word to yourself, you are more likely going to keep your word with others as well. All of this starts from the inside. You have probably heard the saying, "Happiness is an inside job." I believe "Integrity is an inside job," as well. You generate respect with yourself as well as from others. It takes a lifetime to build one's character, yet a moment to lose it. The choice is completely yours.

Summary

The three components of authenticity: 1) self-acceptance, 2) not worrying about what others think, and 3) maintaining a level of personal integrity, are all important in achieving and maintaining self-esteem. As you can see in the examples given, they all tie in with each other. You can have self-esteem with each of them, yet if you combine all of the principles, your self-esteem will soar far above what you thought possible.

You are a very important and powerful being. You truly always have the choice to live authentically in any moment. You have the choice to feel clarity in every decision you make and attain that sense of freedom that being you can bring. Be proud of who you are, don't worry about what others think, and strive to maintain a high level of personal integrity. In doing so, you can find the greatest feeling of pride, love, and self-esteem. Follow your heart and your own path. Choose to live your life, your dream. You can do whatever it is you put your mind toward and be completely unstoppable. See the greatness within yourself and choose to live the authentic you. Make your life awesome. Take the worthwhile journey and do it now! You know how they put that tiny little dash between the year you were born and year you die? Well, what are you doing with your dash? I say you make it come alive! Make your dash an exclamation point! Make an authentic, awesome life for yourself! You are worth it!

About
Jordana Tiger

Jordana Tiger, M.A., M.F.T., Certified Professional Co-Active Coach (C.P.C.C.), is an award winning public speaker and founder of Awesome Life Coaching, a company specializing in personal development and success. She is a Certified Life Coach who assists others to achieve complete fulfillment in their lives. Her personal coaching helps to unlock the door for you in regards to your passion and purpose in life. She will help you clarify your values and assist you to see that choice is a powerful word and in your reach. She helps you find balance so you have a life of quality, and she gets you to see you can change obstacles into limitless possibilities. She works with you in being authentic with yourself; therefore, tapping into your own amazing power. She inspires and motivates you to be completely unstoppable in your transformation and commitment to having an awesome life. Jordana can help you increase your overall personal effectiveness and satisfaction, help you set a structure for organization, and keep you accountable for what you say you are up to in life. She will hold you bigger than you at times hold yourself. She will believe in you and keep you headed in a forward direction.

Jordana has coached athletes in the past and now coaches individuals looking for a positive change and greater freedom and success. She works with educators, small business owners, new coaches, and individuals that feel 'stuck' and are going through some type of transition in their life. She also works with many individuals who have Attention Deficit Disorder. In her psychotherapy practice she works with individuals on many issues such as addition/recovery issues, adults who were abused as children, communication between couples, families of special needs children, and HIV/AIDS issues.

Jordana presents workshops and lectures on many topics including life balance, values, and achieving self-esteem through living an authentic life.

Jordana is also a State Credentialed Teacher who works with special needs children, as well as their families. She is a member of the International Coach Federation, Professional Mentors Coaches Association, California Association of Marriage and Family Therapists, Toastmasters International, Business Alliance of Los Angeles, and California Association of Physical Education, Health, Recreation, and Dance.

To reach Jordana, email her at JT@AwesomeLifeCoaching.com, visit her website at www.AwesomeLifeCoaching.com, or call her at (818) 558-9162.

Eight Steps
to Authentic Self-Expression

by Marilyn French Hubbard

My professional work with self-esteem began as a leadership development trainer being retained by individuals and corporations to teach the skills needed to be assertive rather than passive or aggressive. Clients wanted to learn how to get along with others so they could accomplish their personal and professional goals. They wanted to learn how to express their true feelings, to learn how to say no when they wanted to say no, instead of saying yes. Many clients felt they were viewed as pushovers and others felt they were viewed as bullies. I constantly heard the complaint, "I always get taken advantage of," "Nobody ever listens to me," or "I always make a fool out of myself and feel bad later."

While clients were eager to get right to the skill-building part of the assertiveness training program so they could develop better relationships and interactions with others, it became clear to me that they needed coaching on how to develop better relationships with themselves. The question I kept asking myself was, "How can I support them in being proactive instead of reactive?" Although many of my clients were gainfully employed in corporations or successful entrepreneurs, they knew they were not reaching their full potential. I often heard the comment, "Something is missing." Although they appeared to have it all together on the outside, it quickly became apparent to me that there were internal issues such as doubts, fears, guilt, shame, or feelings of inferiority or inadequacy. I interpreted their quest for assertiveness as a request for authentic self-expression. I knew no growth, change, or transformation could occur until these "self" issues were addressed: self-rejection, self-denial, and self-sacrificing. While I saw self-esteem as the underlying issue, I also knew the issues of self-acceptance, self-trust, self-love, self-value, self-commitment, and self-affirmation had to be enhanced.

In our coaching sessions, I would remind those clients that to face life with low self-esteem is to be at a severe disadvantage because it alters the way you see yourself, and the way you respond to others. During the coaching process they began to see that the better they felt about themselves, the more likely they were willing to take risks or express themselves authentically or assertively. Their authentic self-expression increased as their view of their feelings, thoughts, and actions became consistent with their vision of the future for themselves. Client after client reported that they had begun to accomplish some of their goals through their self-expression; by using their God-given talents, skills, and abilities to start businesses; to get promotions; and through artistic and other creative endeavors.

For example, a client, Barbara, shared that she had made her financial dream come true, that she more than doubled her income. She had gained the courage to authentically express herself and to take a stand on an issue in her community that she felt strongly about. When a community coalition received foundation funding, they immediately offered her the position of Executive Director. She attributed some of her success to our coaching relationship and her ability to take more risk and to express herself authentically.

Eight Steps to Authentic Self-Expresssion

Eight Steps to Authentic Self Expression is a coaching process to enhance authentic self-expression. The journey has pathways of self-acceptance, self-acknowledgment, self-discovery, self-protection, self-discipline, self-expression, self-giving, self-renewal, and self-esteem. On the journey, clients are coached to engage in introspection, reflection, transformation, and action on each pathway.

The self-guided journey can be traveled alone or with a supportive group of individuals. Once clients have traveled the journey for themselves, they are equipped to self-monitor, stay the course, and profoundly impact the lives of others along the way.

Each of the Eight Steps to Authentic Self-Expression is the foundation for the next step. The eight steps are: Seeing,

Surrendering, Shifting, Simplifying, Structuring, Supporting, Sharing, and Shaping the Future. The first two steps are designed to promote discovery or to lighten the load or the baggage that may be weighing the client down. Steps three through five help the client determine action, or travel with ease, and to pack new bags. Steps six through eight assist the client in removing barriers or roadblocks and to stay on course.

When I first met Barbara, she was employed as a senior clerk at an automotive supply company. She was living with the fear of losing her job because the company was considering downsizing. She wanted a better paying job, but she said she was settling for what she had because she had not finished her college degree. She had been using the lack of money and her poor credit rating as the reason she could not accomplish some of her goals. She said she was in debt. However, she didn't know how much because she couldn't bear to open up her bills because she didn't want to deal with knowing what a failure she was. She believed in going to church, but kept going from church to church because she couldn't find a church where the people were friendly. Her coworkers called her "shy" because she wouldn't talk much, but she said she was embarrassed and afraid to talk or be around important people because she felt intimidated by people who made more money or had a better education than she had. She said she was jealous of some of her girlfriends because they seemed to have more fun in their lives than she did.

Barbara and I entered a coaching relationship with the focus to improve her self-esteem. During our coaching relationship, I took Barbara through the following Eight Steps to Authentic Self-Expression, as illustrated on the next page.

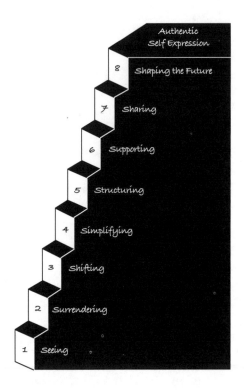

EIGHT STEPS TO AUTHENTIC SELF-EXPRESSION

Step 1 - Seeing: The Truth Shall Set You Free

Seeing, the first step on the journey to authentic self-expression, requires introspection. The purpose of Seeing is to assist clients in gaining a deeper level of self-awareness and consciousness about the current circumstances existing in their lives. Not seeing or not knowing keeps us immobile. Seeing is a process of awakening and observing, not judging, the lives we have created for ourselves. Seeing is not looking at what was or what could be. It's looking at the reality of what is actually going on. Seeing is coming out of the darkness and into the light. It requires opening our eyes and closely examining our life, lifestyle, and livelihoods. Life is based on the inner self, lifestyle is based on the external self, and livelihood is based on the skills, talents, and abilities we use to create the resources required to sustain us. The goal is to examine all three areas to develop a deeper level of self-understanding, self-respect, and self-trust.

Barbara was requested to ask and answer the following questions:

Step 1 – Seeing

- What might be preventing you from seeing the truth?
- What price have you paid for not knowing?
- What are your God-given talents, skills, and abilities?
- When are you most fearful?
- When are you most courageous?

Step 2 - Surrendering: Let Go, Let God

Surrendering, the second step on the journey to authentic self-expression, requires reflection and is designed to assist the client in expanding their self-forgiveness and self-acceptance. Clients are coached to stop being a victim, to stop beating themselves up for their past mistakes, and to dismantle all unempowering self-images by seeking to expand awareness and the willingness to see and correct mistakes. Letting go and accepting frees space to allow new and exciting things to come into your life. To surrender is essential to freeing you from unnecessary shackles, breaking free, and moving beyond limited thinking, behaviors, and actions. Not letting go keeps us a prisoner of our past. Reflecting on past mistakes, making peace with them, and applying the lessons learned are part of the forgiveness, healing, and self-acceptance process. The willingness to ask for help and guidance, not because the person is weak, but because they want to remain strong, is encouraged. Surrendering includes self-acknowledgement of strengths and weaknesses, the recognition that they have not only had defeats, but victories, too. Surrendering is acknowledging and responding to not only fears and doubts, but also, hopes and dreams. To surrender is a state of knowing that the power is within self, not outside of self.

Barbara was requested to ask and answer the following questions:

STEP 2 - SURRENDER

- What might be preventing you from acknowledging the truth?
- What matters to you?
- What would happen if you allowed yourself to think and act differently?
- What do you need to forgive yourself for?
- What are you committed to?

Step 3 - Shifting: The Be-Do-Have Paradigm

Shifting, the third step to authentic self-expression, requires the willingness to acknowledge, embrace, and pursue your aspirations. Shifting requires knowledge of your value and worth and taking personal responsibility for the quality of your life. It is a commitment to settle for nothing less than quality and excellence. Shifting is an inner journey of self-discovery and self-responsibility, a mental shift, for example, from a poverty consciousness to a prosperity consciousness. Shifting is a mindset to *be* committed to *have* what you want. On this path, you don't have to *"do"* anything. You have to *be* something, to *have* what you desire. You have to *be* open to *being* all you can become. You have to *be* authentic and willing to express your feelings. Know that you have personal human rights and speak up for your rights when it's appropriate. Help yourself develop more self-confidence, disagree when you think it is important, and carry out plans for modifying your own behavior. Authentic self-expression, a continual process of becoming, is having the courage to be who you are in all situations.

Shifting is a process of looking at the gap between where you are and where you want to be and being willing to improve your strengths and modify areas that may be affecting your personal effectiveness. Shifting may require reinventing yourself. As shifts and growth happen, clients behave differently and are engaged in a life with authentic self-expression.

Barbara was requested to ask and answer the following questions:

Step 3 - Shifting

- What thoughts, actions, and behaviors may *not* be bringing you the results you desire?
- In what situations do you feel most comfortable in standing up for yourself?
- Where have you not lived up to your full potential?
- In what situations do you say "yes" when you really want to say "no"?
- What price have you paid for living up to someone else's expectations?

Step 4 - Simplifying: Achieving Harmony in Your Life

Simplifying, the fourth step on the journey to authentic self-expression, is a balancing act that is driven by your aspirations, hopes, and dreams. Simplifying helps you to sharpen your focus so you can align your actions and activities with well-stated intentions to support your desired outcomes. There are 12 key areas of Simplifying. One area out of alignment will have an impact on the others. When roles conflict with each other, it drains time, energy, resources, and feelings of self worth.

The twelve key areas of Simplifying are:

- **Personal**: the relationship you have with yourself.
- **Interpersonal:** the relationships and interactions with others.
- **Organizational**: the ability to organize people, build teams, solve problems, and create aligned vision, goals, structure, strategy, and systems.
- **Spiritual**: the inner essence, deeper meaning, and purpose in life; provides the foundation for the development of the other levels.
- **Mental/Educational**: the intellect, our ability to think and reason, thoughts, attitudes, ideas, view points, beliefs, values, and basic life philosophy.
- **Emotional**: the ability to experience life deeply and to relate to others and the world on a feeling level.
- **Physical**: the ability to manage your physical well being.

- **Political**: the awareness and involvement in the social and political issues that are of interest.
- **Legal**: obeying the law and acting as an example for your children and other family members.
- **Technical**: staying current in a technologically changing world.
- **Social:** the reminder that fun is important.
- **Environmental:** the world around you, including your home, car, and office.

Feeling unconfident in any of these areas can have an impact on your self-esteem and authentic self-expression.

Within each area, look at where you are versus where you want to be, then develop goals to fill the gap in each area. Achievement of personal goals can have an enormous impact on your self-esteem. Measurement of your progress in each area is a must. Many paths on the journey may arrive at the same destination. But, to stay on the path and avoid detours, you must be as specific as possible and make sure that the path you follow suits all aspects of your life. The ultimate goal is integration of all aspects of life and to find balance at all levels. When all levels are in balance, a sense of well being and authentic self-expression appears.

Barbara was requested to ask and answer the following questions:

Step 4 - Simplifying

- Which of the twelve areas do you feel most confident about?
- Do you feel more comfortable fitting in or standing out in a crowd?
- Where does your source of security and safety come from?
- How would you feel if you had the courage to be who you really are?
- What goals do you need to accomplish to make your vision of yourself a reality?

Step 5 - Structuring: A Frame for Your Life

Structuring, the fifth step on the journey to self-esteem, is the self-discipline to translate insights, understandings, and awareness into purposeful, meaningful, constructive actions. Structuring helps you plot the route to authentic self-expression. Structuring makes you accountable. You are an expert in your life. You, and only you, can develop your own standards of acceptability and monitor yourself to see if your standards are too high or too low. You put the necessary order, structure, and discipline into life to give you the self-control needed to empower yourself. Daily habits and rituals like prayer, meditation, exercising, preparation, listening, relationship-building, and ongoing self understanding are maintenance activities that contribute to your self-esteem and authentic self-expression. While these activities may seem easy to push aside, they are exactly the things that will make the difference in the results produced.

Keeping your word to yourself is a main ingredient in self-esteem. Through the fulfillment of promises and commitments that you keep to yourself, you will start to generate a sense of self-trust. Meeting deadlines, or completing what you started because you gave your word to do so enhances self-trust. By putting structure in your life, you have a clear-cut, day–to-day method of reviewing your progress.

Barbara was requested to ask and answer the following questions:

Step 5 - Structuring

- What are you trying to achieve?
- What feedback systems have you put in place to indicate your progress?
- What new information do you need to consider?
- How do you get there from here?
- What incomplete business do you need to make complete?

Step 6 - Supporting: Having Company on Your Journey

Supporting, the sixth step on the journey to self-esteem, is an opportunity to gain an interdependent network of other people who can give you feedback and who support you along the path to authentic self-expression. This network should consist of people who want success for you as badly as you want it for yourself; people who are going to be there for you when we need them; people who will see the greatness in you when you may not be able to see the greatness in yourself; people who will hold you accountable for whom you say you want to be; people who will not judge you, but encourage you to continue to let your voice be heard. Supporting will give you the opportunity to gain from and contribute to the knowledge and experience of others.

Most of us are afraid to share our ideas, hopes, and dreams because we fear other people will laugh at us, tell us it won't work, or perhaps steal our dreams. We may have these fears because we have not surrounded ourselves with the right people. Support comes in various ways, shapes, and forms from people, places, and things. In addition to a trusting coaching relationship, other people on the support team you establish can be lovers, challengers, backers, role models, friends, mentors, mentees, like-minded, opposites, allies, and celebrators. In order to receive support you also have to be willing to give it.

Coaches are people who help you chart out your behavior, not based upon your past, but what you want for the future. They help you determine "what's missing" and develop a plan to find the missing piece to the puzzle. They allow you to choose what course of action is best for you. For a coaching relationship to be successful, seek out a coach who models the assertive behaviors you desire. For the coaching relationship to be successful, you have to be "coachable," which requires that you are open to giving and receiving feedback.

The kind of support you most likely have had in the past came from people who agree with you, no matter what. Also, you may have tried to get all of your support from one person, perhaps your significant other or a parent. As you grow and evolve, sometimes you outgrow your supporters in certain areas. To gain the support of others, you have to share what you are doing, so they can assist you. When you are expressing yourself authentically and naturally, you will begin to fully live your life. Build a network of people who are honest and competent to give feedback and who understand your dreams and commitments.

Barbara was requested to ask and answer the following questions:

Step 6 - Supporting

- How would you treat yourself if you were a best friend to yourself?
- What areas do you need the most support in, now?
- Who are you going to request support from?
- How and when will you request support?
- Who are you going to offer your support to?

Step 7 - Sharing: The More You Give, The More You Get

Sharing, the seventh step on the journey to authentic self-expression, is the act of self-giving. Practice being generous with yourself by giving others the gift of your presence. Giving of yourself and knowing that your contribution made a difference in someone's day or life enhances your self-esteem. Give to others by setting the example of walking the talk and being honest about challenges and how you overcame them. Share your voice and speak out on causes in your community that you feel passionately about. Allowing yourself to be collaborative with others around a shared purpose or cause gives you skills in resolving conflicts and building synergy. Be a contributor. Practice listening and really hearing what others are saying. Don't be afraid to hold your head up and look them straight in the eye when you speak.

Give emotionally to others. Open yourself up to being there for others. Be present. Allow others their opportunity to share themselves with you. One of the best actions you can perform in relation to giving and receiving is to keep a gratitude journal of all things you are grateful for. Write in it every day as a discipline. Sharing your gratitude for how much you are progressing on your journey is an act of authentic self-expression. Your authentic self-expression allows you an opportunity to communicate to others your unique knowledge, skills, experience, and talent. By sharing yourself with others and with your community, you enrich everyone, including yourself.

Barbara was requested to ask and answer the following questions:

Step 7 - Sharing

- What are you most grateful for?
- What example do you want others to follow?
- What aspect of your life do you enjoy sharing most?
- What relationship does sharing have with receiving?
- What is the greatest gift you have ever received?

Step 8 - Shaping the Future: We're All One

Shaping the Future, the eighth step to authentic self-expression, is about renewal and transformation. The world is in a place where we desperately need people who will stand up and let their authentic voices be heard with a high level of self-acceptance, self-responsibility, and self-assertiveness. Together we can help transform the world. There is a renewed awakening throughout the world for people with increased self-esteem who speak and act with honesty and integrity. We all want the same thing for our families, our communities, and ourselves. We want to be treated fairly and justly. We want to feel safe and secure and experience the freedom of knowing that we won't be punished for admitting, "I made a mistake," or for saying, "I don't know."

When more people feel accepted and treated with courtesy, listened to, and invited to express their thoughts and feelings, more authentic voices will be heard. When more people feel recognized and acknowledged for the diversity of their individual contributions and achievements, we'll all feel proud. Together we can create a better future when, individually and then collectively, we make the commitment to continuously work on our own self-esteem and to raise the level of consciousness of those around us. The path to getting from where you are to where you want to be is a lifetime journey. Most important, whether the changes we want to make in our lives come quickly or take a little longer, we need to accept and love ourselves just the way we are. We are who we are, unique human beings with unique God-given gifts and unique experiences. Let your voice be heard.

Barbara was requested to ask and answer the following questions:

STEP 8 – SHAPING THE FUTURE

- What is your personal calling?
- How can you support others in speaking their truth?
- What unique gifts do you bring to the world?
- How are you *being*?
- Where do you go from here?

During the coaching process and after answering the questions asked of her, Barbara started talking to herself differently. She stopped comparing herself to others. She started opening her bills and communicating with her creditors. She discovered that having poor credit did not mean that she was a poor person. She stopped seeing herself as *less than* and started affirming herself for her uniqueness. She realized that although she didn't have a college degree, she did have a powerful voice. Her coworkers commented that she even started looking better and walking with more pep to her step. She started volunteering at church and was pleasantly surprised that people were actually listening to her and amazed at all of the new friends she made. Barbara became very involved with her neighborhood revitalization project. Consequently, she was eventually appointed as the Executive Director of the Coalition of Neighborhood Clubs in her community.

By using a coach and through her willingness to apply the principles presented to her, Barbara has transformed her life. She has gained the courage to express herself, and with her increased self-esteem, has not only changed her life, but is changing the lives of those around her. This is the true beauty of taking the Eight Steps to Authentic Self-Expression.

About
Marilyn French Hubbard

As an author, business coach, speaker, facilitator, and senior-level corporate executive, Marilyn French Hubbard, Ph.D., M.C.C., combines her formal education, business experience, and on-going personal growth with her commitment to support individuals and organizations as they create their desired futures. Marilyn is a pioneer and an authority on entrepreneurial and transformational leadership. She assists individuals with bringing focus into their lives and creating their livelihoods by discovering their God-given gifts and talents. She coaches business leaders to embrace diversity and to nurture the human resources within their organizations. She believes there is a link between health, wealth, and spirituality, and that true leaders serve others.

Marilyn's interest in the economic empowerment of women led her to become the founder of the National Association of Black Women Entrepreneurs, a 5,000 member international network for entrepreneurial and enterprising women. Marilyn has inspired and coached thousands of women pursuing their entrepreneurial dreams. Because of her leadership and advocacy on behalf of women and minorities, she has served as an advisor to Michigan governors and mayors, and to the administrations of Presidents Bill Clinton, George H. Bush, Ronald Reagan, and Jimmy Carter.

In her first business book, *Sisters are Cashing In* (2000, Perigee, ISBN 0-399-52572-6), Marilyn integrates business and spiritual principles and offers insights into the emotional, mental, and spiritual factors that can lead you into debt and poverty. She also presents strategies to break negative patterns and help you discover the kind of freedom, wealth, and power that come from having your life in order, doing what you love for a living, and making a contribution to the success of others.

Marilyn is on the senior leadership team and is the Corporate Vice President for Organization and Community Partnerships with the Henry Ford Health System in Detroit, Michigan. She is accountable for aligning the System's mission, vision, and values with its commitment to corporate responsibility by partnering with Human Resources, Government, and Public Affairs in maintaining a corporate culture that supports the health and well being of their 17,000 employees. She also works to create external partnerships that are economically, socially, and environmentally healthy for the community.

Marilyn is a graduate of Ferris State University, The University of Detroit-Mercy, Central Michigan University, and the American Institute. She is certified as a Master Certified Coach by the International Coach Federation.

To contact Marilyn, send an email to MFHubbard@aol.com, or visit the National Association of Black Women Entrepreneurs, Inc. website at www.NABWE.com.

Achieving Selfhood Through Self-Esteem©

by Laurie Sheppard

We all want to experience self-esteem because it underlies our sense of who we are, confirming our choices and actions. But self-esteem is not an end in itself; it is the prime contributor to our evolvement as a fully developed self—of achieving *selfhood*.

Selfhood is the state of being an individual personality (or distinct identity), and of being self-centered. I don't mean self-centered in a selfish, ego pursuit, but in a positive, purposeful way, self-reliant, self-controlled, and self-loving. The longing we feel nudging us onward to "get there" in our life is our need to connect with our selfhood, where we experience refuge and strength. Achieving selfhood is the desired maturation process of any human being. Recognizing and maintaining our self-esteem supports our human need to be received and understood by others and to realize our contribution. Self-esteem allows us to acknowledge our value and appreciation for our self and our life and in doing so returns us to that state of selfhood. *But what is keeping us from that?*

The following five topics touch on ways to expand ourselves so that we have an intimate knowledge of who we are, what our preferences are, and how to fulfill our goals confidently. The topics are accompanied by key questions we can use to try a new path before following old familiar patterns of behavior. They are not intended to be a summary of all issues pertaining to self-esteem or quick fixes. However, any one of the topics presented here, if pursued by a reasonably optimistic individual with openness for a full experience, will carry them further in meeting the challenges of finding their identity and achieving a positive outlook.

"IT'S THE POINT OF YOUR VIEW THAT DECIDES WHAT YOU SEE – ONE MAN'S FLOP IS ANOTHER MAN'S HIT...DEPENDING UPON WHERE YOU SIT."

~ BETTE MIDLER ~

Knowing Oneself and One's Drivers

As we go through life, we have thoughts and feelings we associate with our experiences. We interpret the facts from countless recollections, and use those to form views of our self and our world. Those views become the basis for our behavior and development and they drive our choices. One detour on the journey to connect with our selfhood is not truly knowing our present self because of the filter of those views.

The Little Train That Could is the story of a train ill-equipped to make it up a very steep hill carrying passengers beyond its normal load. That was the big train's job, but the big train had broken down. To help the delayed passengers, the smaller train agreed to carry everyone over the other side of the steep hill and, huffing and puffing, it managed to do just that. In life, we often meet challenges in a very similar way. We take tasks on whether we're capable of them or not, sometimes without any clear reason. We then experience doing it successfully or struggling with the failure. When we cannot do what we want, we often say something is wrong and we feel disconnected or inept. Perhaps we were able to do it once, but another time we were not. Regardless, our "failure" to perform as we expect can cause us to judge ourselves, and often we feel a loss of self-esteem. The little train didn't look at its history of hauling lighter loads to know whether it was capable of pulling the bigger load up the hill. It simply was willing to try to make it and learn its capabilities along the way. This is certainly one way of accomplishing results. However, in doing so, have we actually learned something about ourselves? To move ourselves forward we must learn lessons when they present themselves.

Part of our task then, is to be consistently reinforcing our sense of self and awareness of new potential. My friend Mark, says, "There are miracles every day!" He's undergoing chemotherapy for cancer and I marvel at how he starts each new day with renewed hope for his journey.

Another way of knowing our self is periodically reviewing what is most important in our life, career, and relationships, and identifying where our strengths and capabilities are in relation to those. As a coach, I have often assisted my clients in assessing their current knowledge of themselves. I combine assessments with specific questions so the client can both see where they are and gauge their readiness and abilities in making certain changes. Without clear identifiers pointing the way, changes will be a reaction to either *external dictates* (such as one's availability, the persuasion of others, rewards offered), or *internal dictates* (such as the need for ego gratification, feeling obliged to perform, or forcing a decision for the sake of movement of any kind). Following those dictates, one often experiences too much pushing or pulling trying to make something happen, like tugging the train up the hill. That can cause a painful sacrificing of one's fundamental self.

What makes sense then is continually taking time to learn about our self and what is currently driving our choices. That knowledge will help us make choices best suited for us. Of course, we cannot possibly know everything about our self in advance of making every choice. Yet, it is the combined knowledge we gain from our inner and outer experiences that teach us who we are and offers us our greatest power for self-control. The East Indian guru and yogic master, Paramahansa Yogananda, said, "The Western day is nearing when the inner science of self-control will be found as necessary as the outer conquest of Nature." He also said, "True knowledge is always power." This knowing of self is a key attribute of self-esteem.

What we base our choices on is fundamental to our selfhood. When challenges and decisions face us, I recommend that before acting we ask ourselves: *"What is driving this choice for me?"*

Sometimes in examining our careers, we may say money and recognition are important. There is nothing wrong with those *drivers* and we can of course get involved in work to satisfy those values. However, over time, those values may not continue to provide sufficient fuel to ignite our passions, keep us fully and deeply engaged, and keep us centered. We need to re-examine where the train is headed and ask if it is still important to go where our current efforts are taking us.

Alicia was spending yet another late night at the company. She was making changes in the financial report she would be discussing tomorrow with accounting. She worked in a busy, creative design department and even though it was not her area to cross-check those figures, she had her fingers in a lot of pots. The recognition she received was what had kept her going the past few years. She was a top manager. She had climbed the corporate ladder rather quickly, making some personal sacrifices in working hard to get there. But more and more, it seemed no matter how hard she worked or how many late nights she spent for the company, the work just piled up and more seemed to be expected of her. Lots of travel had been added to her responsibilities and she began to tire of her position. She realized she didn't really have much of a home life.

Alicia felt she had lost control of her life and mostly of herself. Somewhere along the line her primary career objectives had been driven to achievement, yet she'd failed to give attention to other important areas. Through a written life assessment we reviewed together, Alicia saw her work now as more of a "footnote to her life." Her experience of burnout resulted from not addressing her self-care. Her primary focus then, became reconnecting with her selfhood through honoring her needs first, before those of certain expectant family members and the company. In clarifying her life and career values, Alicia saw how important it was for her to take certain steps to ensure a more balanced future with less push or pull. We laid out a plan for her to act on what she was willing to commit to change.

For Alicia, these obstacles had not been in the forefront as much as her original thought to stay or leave her company, which she thought would alleviate her stress. Alicia gained a deeper knowledge of what "balance" meant for her. She decided to stay with her company for financial reasons, but renegotiate her workload responsibilities. She took various health measures, including creating new friendships and exercise partners. She began to build relationships that nurtured her in return. She was ready to live a life that included a more rewarding list of drivers and at the top of the list was attention to self.

"IN THIS WORLD IT IS NOT WHAT WE TAKE UP,
BUT WHAT WE GIVE UP THAT MAKES US RICH."
~ HENRY WARD BEECHER ~

Measuring and Distractions

Janet stood in front of her supervisor, unable to find the right words to question the restrictions he was placing on this year's training programs. As in-house consultant for a large product development department, Janet had several ideas she wanted to discuss with him. His budget approvals didn't take into account the proposal she'd sent to him over two weeks ago. She began to second-guess that proposal and wondered if it was lacking thoroughness in some way. Staring at his resolute face and listening to the same budget discussion she'd heard before, she felt there wasn't room for her comments. In two subsequent exchanges with him the same week, she tried to exude more confidence in restating her opinion, still without the response she'd hoped for. She began to doubt herself.

Janet was confused by her situation. She usually considered herself pretty confident and forthright in her communications. She told me she was experiencing low self-esteem. She said, "The harder I try to be understood, the less I feel it works." First, we took time to honor her feelings of frustration. Then I suggested that she might be behaving much like the kids in the backseat of the car on a trip, always asking, "Are we there yet?" Of course in that moment she had no idea what I was talking about, which was understandable. So, I explained that children often are measuring the process and time it takes to accomplish something and get frustrated ("How long till we get to Grandma's? Are we going to stop to eat soon?"). Because of their measuring and distraction, they miss a lot of what is actually going on along the way. Janet asked, "How does that relate to my self-esteem?"

What keeps self-esteem evasive is our pervasive need to measure it. We are so busy *trying* to be confident we spend too much time sizing up how we're performing while we're still in the very act of performing. "I'm not sure how I feel and I'm wondering if I'm coming across right? I wish I had better self-esteem. I don't think I'm conveying myself confidently enough." Our hyper-vigilance of our self results in a conclusion that something is missing and we don't measure up. We immediately say it shouldn't be this way and question what's wrong with us, the situation, or others. In the process of all this measuring, we say we're either experiencing low self-esteem, having negative self-esteem, or that we've lost it altogether.

My contention is that there is no such thing as low, negative, or even lost self-esteem. At any given time, we either have self-esteem or we don't. We regard ourselves with appreciation and respect, or we negate who we are. Like scientists, we are fascinated with the notion of the tangibility and qualifying of *facts* as we interpret our self. This obsession with self-esteem as a thing to be measured prevents our returning to selfhood.

Janet's time and energy was occupied with thoughts of her upcoming wedding and pending graduate school finals. Her attention was distracted, as she was clearly making some major life changes. Her energy level was low. Both situations were affecting her otherwise confident nature. We often have multiple scenarios occurring. At times, we balance the chaos well; at other times, we find we are distracted from our home base—our selfhood. How we relate to this state of distraction determines our presence, or lack, of self-esteem. Life's details can in themselves be distracting. However, at certain times we are more prone to this than at other times. When we try to bring ourselves back to center, we start by trying to measure how far off center we are. Instead, we simply need to acknowledge our distraction and refocus. In seeing this, Janet was able to start anew in her communication with her supervisor. A question we might ask ourselves when we feel disconnected is this: "How am I being distracted?" As we notice our distractions, we are then able to minimize them and regain focus. We naturally return to what matters to us most.

> "MOST OF THE SHADOWS OF THIS LIFE ARE CAUSED
> BY STANDING ON ONE'S OWN SUNSHINE."
> ~ RALPH WALDO EMERSON ~

Tell Our Truth

Another derailment of self-esteem is not telling the truth about what we really want. There are times when we say lots of things are important to us and we have conflict of interests. For a period, that may be true. However, we become entrapped in a web of confusion of our own making when we subject ourselves to divergent courses of action. If we have reviewed and determined what's most valuable to us, then actions contradicting that will deny our values. We will spend time and energy trying to make new decisions to sort things out, while literally finding ourselves running in several directions.

How often I have heard clients, friends, family (even me) bemoan our busy state of affairs. Yet, we've embarked on conflicting paths in our personal or business lives when we already had prior commitments. The question to ask is: *"What is my truth here?"*

I believe we're afraid to choose one primary goal because we're hedging our bets to be certain that at least one opportunity will pay off. However, it's more risky to disperse our time and energy and possibly miss the pleasure of completing our main objective. It isn't that the dream can't live in the future when scenarios may change. The problem is in trying to do it right now when we've already chosen a particular direction.

Our most often told stories come from our view of how hard it is not to get to do all the things we want, when we want them. We have difficulty accepting we're the one creating the problem as we convince ourselves we're getting the short end of the stick in life. This is a sure sign we don't know ourselves at that moment. Then we expect others to know what we want and support us in getting it. When they don't, we may blame them for the lack of support, or feel we're not worthy of it. In actuality, it's the *mirror effect*. When we don't really know ourselves, others won't either. On the other hand, when we adhere to our own chosen values and respect our self, others will mirror back that clarity and respect. From honoring our self in this way, we'll make correlate choices and feel the strength of our convictions through both inner and outer means.

"WE ARE WHAT WE REPEATEDLY DO.

EXCELLENCE THEN IS NOT AN ACT, BUT A HABIT."

~ ARISTOTLE ~

Discipline of Likeableness

To really love our self and others, as taught to us through religion or spirituality, is one thing. To simply like who we are, is another; and many of us just don't like ourselves. When we're really centered, life feels good; we have a purpose, a mission, and we are energized. When we self-doubt, we feel lifeless and have little passion for anything. We don't take care of ourselves, causing a spiral effect of running ourselves down and often becoming ill. Typically, we close out other's support at these times, too. Catching ourselves before engaging in destructive internal dialogues, is a practice to engage in and improve over time. There may not be complete acceptance at first, but it can at least start with more positive self-communication. For example, it's a better practice to say, "That was stupid," rather than, "I'm so stupid." We must discipline ourselves to have self-assuredness, whether things are going well or not. We do that by simply liking our self just as we are. Imagine this whole self-esteem concept really boiled down to that idea! I suggest we check in with our self periodically and reaffirm our strong suits by asking this question: *"Right now, what's one thing I really like about myself?"*

Periodically, I notice myself feeling needy for attention, affection, or recognition. Intellectually, I recognize the desire as normal, but I also notice confusion can set in because I begin to battle against myself about feeling that way at all. I tell myself I don't like my behavior. Because of that, I begin to feel unsure of myself and am not even comfortable simply being with myself.

In one recent experience, my mind sorted through my current life and looked for something out of place as the cause of this feeling. I focused on something being wrong in my connection with my husband. I was actually creating something wrong by thinking that, since nothing had actually occurred to cause me to think it. I simply felt disconnected with myself, but reacted as if it was a disconnection between us and that we should do something about it. What I ultimately realized was my behavior was a function of my lack of self-worth. That awareness was my first step, but then I wanted to consciously, intellectually, manipulate a behavior adjustment: "Fake it till you make it." As you might expect, it did not work. I was reminded it's important not to deny what I was actually feeling, but also not to act in an attempt to alleviate my concerns at that very moment I was having the feelings.

We often take different actions, trying to alleviate the fear of disconnection, when what we have to do is face it head-on, experience the absence of self-esteem, the feeling of discomfort, the uncertainty, and then move through it. We move through it by not continually reflecting on or going over in our head the same thoughts that keep us stuck. We simply have to be with our self, just as we are, and soon our confidence is restored. The more we do that, the more experience we garner realizing it, and the easier it becomes next time.

Notice too, the pull to create drama or take actions of any kind in reaction to everyday normalcy. It's as if the little child in us gets bored, acts up, and demands we pay more attention. The discipline of likeableness means we need to set a priority of attention to our self and not wait for the child's tantrum to remind us.

This may sound hard, but don't fool yourself. Because something is complex doesn't mean it's difficult. Just as something that's simple may not necessarily be easy. A crossword puzzle is complex, with its across, down, and intersecting words. However, the clues can be easy or difficult. The direction to get from point A to B may be as simple as following a straight line on a map. However, getting there may be difficult because of the peaks and valleys that must be crossed. The idea isn't about getting rid of something about yourself you don't like, but learning to be with yourself as you are. Then you have the freedom, knowledge, and access to make changes.

> "WE ARE ACTUALLY THIS VAST EXPANSE OF FREEDOM,
> BUT WE IDENTIFY WITH UNFREE AND LIMITED OBJECTS AND SUBJECTS…
> NONE OF WHICH IS WHAT WE ARE."
> ~ KEN WILBER ~

The Uncertainty Set Point

I frequently tell my clients to stop putting money in the confidence bank. Remember that fragile piggy bank some of us had as a child? I tell them they have enough confidence for a lifetime and they need to break the bank and use it. I suggest instead that they collect uncertain moments that solidify their confidence.

In a moment of feeling unconfident, confused, or doubtful, recalling a time when we felt similarly uncertain about our self and what we did that changed that experience will reinforce our self-esteem. We can use any experience when we directly and positively impacted the outcome and discovered a way to transition to higher ground. Like weight lifting, where one performs sets to build muscles, remembering a few key stories of personal breakthrough is character building.

Exercise: When experiencing self-doubt or feeling undervalued, you can minimize its impact by having five golden coins in your pocket. You can do this literally and figuratively. Commit to memory a synopsis of five situations in which you can vividly recall an uncertain moment, a moment of intense indecision, a crisis, or an awkward situation in which you felt out of touch with yourself and yet found a way through the problem. At that very point you said something to yourself and then took action that allowed a positive shift in the situation. Feelings accompanied that change and it's important to remember those too as you walk yourself out of a state of disconnection into renewed self-value.

This reminds me of a story, the untold story of the three little pigs. Remember the first two pigs made their homes from straw and sticks and were gobbled up by the hungry wolf. Meanwhile, several different times, the third little pig showed cunning in avoiding the wolf and sparing his own life. That accomplishment should have left him in hog heaven. Instead, the pig began to doubt himself. He imagined the whole experience was just dumb luck. He soon put his attentions on building an even stronger home. He spent much time alone and was unhappy. One day he was cooking up another fine turnip stew, which he had not done in many years. Suddenly, he heard an angry pack of wolves at his door. He was confident they couldn't get in. But, he said to himself, what good is living life this way, when I can't go out? As he stirred the large pot of stew and stroked his whiskers, he suddenly remembered the sounds and sights of the earlier encounter with the big bad wolf. He recalled how and why he had so bravely and calmly dealt with it all. He thought of the words he'd spoken to the angry wolf, "not by the hair of my chinny-chin-chin." He remembered the wolf even became afraid of him! The howling outside his door now became louder and angrier and yet in this moment of uncertainty, through recalling those earlier thoughts and feelings, the pig's confidence was restored. He yanked open the steel door to his cottage and shouted, "you're just in time boys, pull up a chair." The wolves were stunned by the pig's moxie. The story ends with the pig squealing in delight, the wolves sharing in the feast, and all swapping favorite recipes!

> "If we begin with certainties we shall end in doubts;
> but if we begin with doubts and are patient with them,
> we shall end in certainties."
>
> ~ Francis Bacon ~

If we remain in a state of long-term confusion, are questioning our value repeatedly, or feeling depressed, we would certainly receive benefit from therapeutic support to be guided through those self-destructive patterns. There is a lot of outside support available. To assist in determining our areas of self-defeating behaviors, Marilyn J. Sorensen, Ph.D., offers an assessment questionnaire in her book, *Breaking the Chain of Low Self-Esteem*.

Once we are sure we are not a candidate for therapy, yet want to change self-defeating habits and progress to a healthy self-image, we can take steps in that direction. Knowing we all experience degrees of fear, anxiety, confusion, and other self-defeating emotions that at times impact behavior and performance is important. We all periodically experience self-doubt. Staying on the upside of our mental and emotional outlook is achievable. Utilizing a coach for support can give an added perspective, positively affecting our behaviors, relationships, and work, while guiding us toward our own self-coaching tools.

> "THERE'S A STAR ON THE FAR HORIZON
> RISING BRIGHT IN THE AZURE SKY.
> FOR THE REST OF THE TIME THAT YOU'RE GIVEN,
> WHY WALK WHEN YOU CAN FLY HIGH."
> ~ MARY CHAPIN CARPENTER ~

Living fully today, planning for tomorrow, and taking forward actions then becomes our central life script. Approaching life with a deeply rooted connection to selfhood is both renewing and moves us clearly and simply to our *Next Big Thing*—that which is most important for us now, a valued, worthy objective, that challenges and rewards us. Life becomes the "daring adventure" of which Helen Keller spoke when she said, "Security is mostly a superstition. It does not exist in nature…Life is either a daring adventure or nothing." Self-esteem concerns diminish and rather than being selfishly focused, we are able to focus ourselves on contributing to the journey ahead of us all.

About
Laurie Sheppard

Laurie Sheppard, M.C.C., has coached hundreds of entrepreneurs and professionals to discover and get to their next big thing. As a Life Coach and Career Strategist, she assists her clients in life planning, career development, and transitions. Although Laurie started her coaching company, Creating At Will, in 1994, she has been coaching, consulting, and training for over 16 years.

Prior to starting her business, Laurie held positions in administration in the corporate and legal environments. She implemented a successful training program for redirecting Los Angeles inner city at-risk youths. She developed new training procedures for managers for an international seminar program. Laurie has a formal theater background, having attended both UCSB and UCLA and performed on stage and television. She started her company facilitating creative living workshops for professionals who came from a variety of industries.

A certified coach from a leading coach training program, The Hudson Institute of Santa Barbara, Laurie is also certified as a Master Certified Coach by the International Coach Federation (ICF). She currently serves as President of the ICF's global chapter. She is an active member of the Professional Coaches and Mentors Association and, as a graduate Toastmaster, is a frequent speaker on the topic of change and "Achieving Your Next Big Thing." She is author of the double audiotape series, The 3 C's for Effective Living - Change, Creativity, and Communication. Loaded with valuable insights, questions, and exercises, this program has been used by companies and individuals the world over, and is available at her website and at Amazon books online.

Laurie lives in West Los Angeles, but since she coaches primarily by telephone, her clients are worldwide.

To contact Laurie, call (310) 645-2874, send email to laurie@creatingatwill.com, or visit www.creatingatwill.com.

The Power of Spirit

by Diane Menendez

"IF I KNOW THAT IN A REAL AND PROFOUND SENSE YOU AND I ARE ONE
AND ARE BOTH INTEGRAL PARTS OF THE TOTAL ONE,
I TREAT YOU THE SAME WAY I TREAT MYSELF.
IN ADDITION, I TREAT MYSELF WITH LOVE AND RESPECT
BECAUSE I AM PART OF THE TOTAL HARMONY OF THE UNIVERSE."
- LAWRENCE LeSHAN -

As a psychology intern working with people in recovery from trauma, I noticed that people healed and grew when they adopted a spiritual perspective. People learned to look beyond the pain, to see the gift and the value in what they experienced.

Human beings are naturally spiritual. We seek meaning and connection to something greater than ourselves. When we as coaches relate to clients as inherently spiritual, deeply connected beings, we honor the divine in them. Attending to their wholeness—their deep intellectual, emotional, physical, energetic, relational, and spiritual connections—supports profound growth. The development of self-esteem is a key factor in positive self-growth.

The Five Key Spiritual Principles

This chapter focuses on five key spiritual principles that I use with my clients in helping them develop a better relationship with themselves, and the world around them. After a discussion of a principle, I present a series of exercises to help you understand your own thinking about the principle.

Acknowledge Connectedness

Humans live, grow, and die in systems. We are intimately connected to each other. We develop our thoughts, attitudes, and behaviors early in response to the approval or disapproval of others. Connections even survive death. Family rules influence us until we free ourselves to create new ones.

From the spiritual perspective, connectedness forms one of the great givens, and gifts, of life. Even the client's energy, breathing, and hormones naturally become affected by places, spaces, their own thoughts, and other people. Imagining ourselves as separate is an arrogant illusion, although people often choose to act independent to avoid acknowledging how vulnerable they feel. In fact, when children are developing self-esteem, one of the biggest obstacles we place in front of them can be American adults' urgency about being able to "stand on your own two feet," "be tough enough to go it alone." As an antidote, the coach helps clients see the whole picture, recognizing the paradox that separateness and connection, fallibility and greatness, strength and vulnerability are intimately tied to each other.

Exercise 1: Reflection, Awareness, and Action

To change our thinking requires practice, focus, and attention. Record your experiences and observations using journal-writing exercises like those below:

- Look at the World Around You. In the next week, take one action every day to experience your connectedness with other living things. For example, allow yourself to feel a strong sense of love and caring, then look at others' eyes. Notice what you experience.

- Connect With Your Inner Knowing. You are naturally connected to many sources of information. Your intuition is available to you if you allow it to emerge. Sense the essence of the people, music, environment, and books around you. How open are you to acting upon what you sense? What blocks you from sensing? From acting?

- Notice Synchronicities. Create a clear intention for what you want to create or attain during a period of several weeks. Notice what shows up unexpectedly that can work in accordance with your intention.

- Know Your Values. Living a fulfilled life means living out of deep connection with one's values. Identify your top 3-5 values in life. How well are you living out these values at work? At home?

- Understand Your Habits. In practice, your habits are your values. List five daily habits of thinking or behavior you need to change to live out your values.

- Ask Yourself, "How Authentic Am I?" When you avoid telling the truth because you fear people will get angry, you get disconnected from yourself, your inner wisdom. Connecting more with yourself lets you create deeper connections with others. List the people in your life, past and present, you are disconnected from. What is the truth you haven't spoken? What is it that you most need to be heard about right now in your life?

- Understand the RAV Trap. You may be negatively connected with people through needs for Recognition, Approval, or Validation. You can't live your values when you're being driven by needs. When RAV needs drive you, you are disconnecting from a higher purpose you could achieve. During the past two weeks, when have you been driven by RAV?

Suspend Judgments

> "SEEK THE WISDOM OF THE AGES, BUT LOOK AT THE WORLD
> THROUGH THE EYES OF A CHILD."
>
> - RON WILD -

Managers and professionals get paid for becoming highly adept at making judgments: What's a good investment, what's a bad investment? Who's capable and who's not? What's the right plan? Am I good enough, capable enough, worthy enough? These thoughts fill their mental space with plans and stories that interfere with their ability to experience the present. But professionals aren't the only ones who make judgments; we all do.

Chronic attachment to a *judging mind* has a high cost. It often results in low self-esteem as the client relentlessly judges him/herself and finds him/herself wanting, insufficient every time. Some writers have called this tendency "the gremlin," that relentless critic who takes up residence in the client's mind. The gremlin criticizes every performance, points out all the ways the client isn't enough, and generally makes life miserable. Worst of all, the gremlin keeps the client stuck and unable to live in the present. That's too bad, because the point of greatest potential is always right now, in the present. When people spend too much time with their gremlin, dwelling on the past, judging, or living in the future, they miss the beauty and power of the moment. Fulfillment comes when they focus on the here and now.

We experience joy and fulfillment when we let go of the *judge* and embrace the *learner*—or the *lover*—in ourselves through discovering *beginner's mind*. Beginners shift consciousness from "it isn't enough and here's what it could be instead" toward recognizing that "what's here is just right for now."

Exercise 2: Suspending Judgments

- Examine a Judger's Mind. A judging mind sees the world in shades of black or white, in terms of either/or. A judger's mind is reactive, asking:
  What's wrong with this person, the situation, or with me?
  What do I need to do to stay in control?
  Who is to blame; whose fault is it?
  How can I win?
  How can I look good?

  Set a timer so that it sounds on the hour, every hour between 6 a.m. and 10 p.m. When it sounds, write down the specific thoughts you were having. At the end of the week, ask, "How do my habits of mind serve me? Limit me?"

- Practice Beginner's Mind. Beginners see the world freshly, in terms of "both/and" and respond flexibly to what confronts them. A beginner's mind asks questions like:
  What is there to be appreciated here?
  What can I learn?
  What are the choices?
  What am I feeling and experiencing right now?

Set a timer so that it sounds on the hour, every hour between 6 a.m. and 10 p.m. When it sounds, use Beginner's Mind. Write down specifically what occurs.

- Breathe Consciously and Focus on the Present. Use a 4-minute meditation once per hour at work. Sit in a quiet place and focus your attention on your breath. Exhale fully from the deepest place inside your being. Just notice your breath. When distracting thoughts come, notice them and simply return to your breathing.

Replace Fear With Love and Trust

"IF PAIN IS TO BE MEANINGFUL, IT MUST SERVE SOME GREATER PURPOSE. THAT PURPOSE IS THE LIBERATION OF THE SOUL FROM THE ARMOR OF SELF-PROTECTION THAT IS CREATED OUT OF FEAR."

- ANDREW SCHNEIDER -

"I ACCEPT THE UNIVERSE."

- MARGARET FULLER -

When a person learns to suspend judgment, they notice how the mind tricks them into feeling anxious by focusing on the future and making judgments. Research shows that human beings *naturally* fear only three things: falling, high places, and tight spaces. A judger's mind creates fear by focusing on "what if" and imagining a terrible future. Fear causes muscles to contract, so that fearful people experience chronic tension. Obviously, energy that is spent contracting is energy a person could be investing in growth.

When a person can acknowledge the limiting power of fear and can let go, they release themselves from tension that wraps them like a vise. They open up to trusting themselves, others, and experience.

EXERCISE 3: LOVING AND TRUSTING

- Your Relationship Energy. Who are the people around whom you feel most energized? Most calm? Most de-energized? What's the story you tell yourself about them that is de-energizing you?
- Experience Others. How skilled are you at connecting with others well? Can you be close and feel safely vulnerable?

Can you maintain distance without feeling arrogance or anxiety? Rate each of your key work and family relationships. Use a scale of 1 to 10 (1 = distant, 5 = optimal, 10 = merged). What is your pattern?

- Examine Your Fears. When blocked by fear, ask, "What other fears are fueling this one?" Find a root fear, like fear of pain, loss or lack, abandonment/separation/rejection, being of no value/being judged, meaninglessness. Root fears fuel anxiety.
- Connect with Love. Situations that trigger fear are really disguised opportunities for love. Find out what is needed to connect with and love, because love drives out fear.

Notice How You Create Your Reality

"THE MIND IS ITS OWN PLACE AND IN ITSELF
CAN MAKE A HEAVEN OF HELL, A HELL OF HEAVEN."

– JOHN MILTON –

In his book *Illusions,* Richard Bach writes, "The world is your exercise book, the pages on which you do your sums. It is not reality." In that sense, when a person is stuck, they're refusing to learn, to see. Adults don't like to be wrong. So, we create our reality by seeking confirmation for what we've already concluded is true. We make up a story, then forget we created it and come to believe it is truth. (Judging Mind again!)

It's as if a person looks at a situation and sees only one tree, when there's a whole forest image. Notice your power to confuse the story with the truth by asking yourself powerful questions that pull your attention toward alternative views.

EXERCISE 4: ASK YOURSELF POWERFUL QUESTIONS.

- What old idea are you in love with here? Does it still serve you?
- What is the hidden opportunity here?
- How are you wanting to be right?
- What is an important truth about this situation? What's an opposite truth? How are both true?
- What are you focused on that limits your ability to see the whole picture? What have you been ignoring?
- What's the forest? What's the tree you're not noticing?

- How would things change if you faced the fear and acted?
- What difference will this make in 100 years?
- How are you making yourself hopeless, a victim?
- What would someone like Martin Luther King or Groucho Marx do?
- What are you most grateful for?

OTHER EXERCISES

- Cultivate a sense of appreciation and gratitude for everything that shows up in your life. Practice wonder, reverence, and awe daily. These are ways of expressing love. They relieve pain and connect us with joy. Each day this week, end your day by listing 10 things you are grateful for. Do not name anything you named on previous days.

Discover Your Purpose

> "STAY IN THE FLOW, AND THE FLOW WILL
> LEAD YOU TO THE EXTRAORDINARY."
>
> - PHIL JACKSON -

People who have a sense of their purpose lead fulfilling lives. Purpose gives life meaning and guides choices by connecting us with something greater than we are. Once someone knows when they are "on purpose," they know how to renew their joy and commitment. When people's lives and actions are aligned with their purpose, they feel a sense of integrity and a healthy self-esteem.

A person needs to discover that the purpose they've been living from may not be authentic—it may be one they adopted or inherited early on. For example, Patrick, the client in the example at the end of this chapter, originally thought his purpose was to succeed and make money. That wasn't purpose; it was the story he created to drive the fight against his old fears of poverty.

A person doesn't need to *invent* a purpose. The task is to *discover* the purpose they've been living out for many years.

EXERCISE 5: DISCOVER YOUR PURPOSE.

- To discover real purpose, not "pseudo purpose," go back to recover past purpose-full experiences. Identify 10-15 specific times (like one event, one day) of times when you felt fulfilled, "on purpose." Take notes on your thoughts, then track key words and phrases you've written down. Find what is common to most of the stories. From there, create a statement of purpose: 3-5 sentences that express a way of *being*, not what you will *do*.

- Write your purpose on post-its and stick it up in 10 places: your planner, your house, car, office. Each time you encounter a post-it, speak your purpose aloud. Then ask yourself, "How am I living out my purpose at this moment?"

CASE EXAMPLE

Patrick came to coaching as a successful 45-year-old professional project manager, trained as an engineer, but dissatisfied with his lucrative position in the high tech industry. His goal was to "beat his frequent fatigue by becoming better at time management."

Connection: When Patrick identified his four key values measured in comparison with his life, he was shocked to discover how disconnected he was from what he valued most. His choices around his work had disengaged him from what he valued most. He valued community. Yet he worked long hours and traveled so often that he rarely attended professional meetings and seldom got to church, though he knew these gave him positive energy. He began to participate again in his church and community, and restructured his work travel to enable him to honor them. He limited contact with the five people he identified as "energy vampires," and began to spend more time with the four people he called his "energy mentors."

Suspending Judgment. Patrick realized that the tension he felt giving client presentations grew out of his need for Recognition, Approval, and Validation. He began to treat himself as he treated his clients, with forgiveness and compassion. He replaced his negative self-talk and criticisms of his work with positive statements.

Replacing Fear with Trust. When Patrick examined his fears, he learned that his fear of being open at work came from his fear of being judged as "not leadership material." He needed to love the sensitive part of himself as much as he loved his intellect. He learned to do this by noticing and appreciating how the sensitivity of others around him created strong relationships and good performance. When he was able to do this with others, he was ready to do it for himself.

We Create Our Reality. When Patrick examined his natural way of seeing the world, he learned that he was caught up in seeing every situation as a fight, requiring him to personally improve on it, win it, fix it. He decided to experiment with WWRWD ("What Would Robin Williams Do?"), which gave him permission to be creative, be light, and be passionate, too.

Purpose. Patrick's life purpose was "to bring adventure, creativity, joy, and wisdom to my work and to my connections with others." "No wonder I feel off track," he said to me. "My work has become routine, it's lost its adventure for me. My joy's gone." He soon asked for a transfer within the company to a job that allowed him to use less of his project management skills, and more of his ability to create relationships. He had great gifts as a project manager—but in using them, he had gotten off track. Yes, he made a great deal of money. But he wasn't serving his purpose or himself.

Profound Simplicity

A client once shared with me how he made sense of coaching from spirit. "Here's what we've been doing," he said excitedly, handing me an article by Angeles Arrien detailing four spiritual rules for life:

- Show up
- Pay attention
- Tell the truth
- Don't be attached to the results

Remove the difficult obstacles to living and increase your self-esteem by following these profoundly simple spiritual rules.

About
Diane Menendez

Diane S. Menendez, Ph.D., M.C.C., has been coaching and consulting to business leaders and professionals for more than 15 years. As a Life Coach, she does both personal and business coaching—because success at work is deeply connected to success at life.

Her qualifications include years of formal education and more time than she sometimes likes to claim in life, business, family, post-graduate, and professional experience. She's worked inside two Fortune 100 companies for 10 years. At AT&T she coached managers to lead teams and develop themselves into flexible, farsighted, and caring leaders who could draw the best out of those they led.

Since 1988, she's been a coach to executives and professionals, working with those who want more satisfaction, more results, more resilience, more balance between work and life, and more ease and effortlessness about their lives. She's been reorganized, promoted five times, downsized once—so she knows a lot about transition in business and in life. She's led organizations and has been led by others—some were great leaders and some, well, not so great. She's owned two businesses and has been in a family business. She knows first-hand that the challenges entrepreneurs and business leaders face demand a great deal from them: courage, willingness to be truthful with themselves and others, and flexibility in experimenting with new ways of being and doing. She has coached 350 + people—leaders, professional women, career changers, entrepreneurs, people in transition, family business owners, and others.

She loves being a partner for people who want to meet the challenges that face them—with zest and grace. Her e-zine series, *The Seamless Life,* can be found on her website at www.HeartDance.org/articles. Her current special interest is how to use our workplaces as vehicles for spiritual development and renewal. She chairs the Special Interest Group, *Healing the Corporate Spirit,* an on-line community within *The Association for Spirit at Work.*

For two years, Diane wrote a column, "Outside the Comfort Zone," which appeared in regional business weeklies. She serves on the Board of the Cincinnati Organization Development Network and convenes the Coaching Salon, a learning and discussion forum for managers and others who coach inside organizations. Her graduate and post-graduate work is in counseling psychology, education, and organization development.

Diane lives in Cincinnati, Ohio. You can contact her by sending an email to Diane@HeartDance.org or by visiting her website at www.HeartDance.org.

You Are What You Think You Are

by Phyllis Sisenwine

After Fred Astaire's first screen test in 1933, he received a memo from the testing director that said, "Can't act! Slightly bald! Can dance a little." He kept that memo over his fireplace for years. The great opera tenor Enrico Caruso's parents wanted him to be an engineer. His teachers said he had no voice and could not sing. Beethoven was very awkward with the violin. His teacher called him hopeless. So often, we are given negative messages. Fortunately for us, these three geniuses did not believe their critics. They told themselves they had talent and proved to the world that they did.

What gives some people confidence and others so much fear about taking risks and succeeding? What is it that Astaire, Caruso, and Beethoven had that propelled them to the heights of their genius? Do you allow the voices you hear—your own and others—to influence what you become? As with Astaire, Caruso, and Beethoven, your choice becomes your reality. You are what you think you are.

Do you still hear negative messages from childhood? Did a teacher say you couldn't write? You're clumsy? You're lazy? Did a parent doubt that you would succeed? I don't believe anyone intentionally sets out to affect someone else's self-esteem, but through negative messages, it happens often.

Of course, we don't need negative messages from other people to lower our self-esteem and stop us from doing what we dream. We often give *ourselves* those negative messages. Like computers, whatever messages we give our brain, it believes. It has no choice. People often hire me as a coach because they want to grow a business or improve their life. Very often lack of self-esteem is their biggest block. They repeatedly tell themselves: "I can't earn the amount of money I want, I'll never get that promotion, I'll never lose weight, or meet my soul mate." One negative message after another. So, I work with clients to change their thoughts, because in order to attract success they must have a positive belief in themselves. Whatever you think about yourself becomes your experience. As Henry Ford said, "If you think you can or you think you can't you're right."

Comparing Yourself to Externals

What thoughts affect your feelings of self worth and your self-talk? One thought is comparing yourself to a person or an external standard (for example, income). For example, I was an outside sales representative for more than twenty years, winning many sales contests and earning a six-figure income. Ironically, my motivation was low self-esteem. My income became my report card. If I earned six figures, I must be okay. However, when money is your self worth, there is never enough. Once I recognized this and started working on increasing my self-esteem internally and not externally, I began to feel worthy, not because of the money, but because I started to believe in my worth as a person. I eventually felt confident enough to leave my sales position, and after a short time off, was encouraged to become a coach. I realized that it was my calling and began coach's training and soon started a coaching business.

Within a short time, the gremlins came out and I started to feel that competitive drive I had when I was in sales. I started thinking, "If I get a lot of clients, then I'll be a good coach." I worked hard and built a practice quickly. One day, while speaking with my own coach, I said I was working hard, but didn't feel successful. He asked, "What is success?" I responded, "A successful coach earns six figures." And my wise coach said, "No, Phyllis, a successful coach has a great life." That was a powerful statement to me. I realized that my low self-esteem was surfacing. I let the financial goals go and worked on modeling a great life. My self-esteem rose, my coaching became more enjoyable for me, clients were attracted to me, and my practice grew even more without my focus on the income.

Through all of this, the biggest change for me has been positive self-talk. I start my day by telling myself that I will have a great day filled with love, joy, and appreciation. Self-love is the greatest motivator for high self-esteem. For so many years I compared myself to others and I usually came up short. Whether they were thinner, prettier, smarter, better athletes, or any other comparison I could think of, I always felt "less than." I focused on what I was lacking, rather than what I had.

To change your self-talk, focus on your positive qualities. Create positive messages to yourself. Write them down and post them around your home. What is your attitude about yourself? Do you still hear the negative voices? Is your attitude about yourself positive or negative? Remember that you are what you think. If you believe you can do something, you are much closer to getting there. If you hear yourself saying, "I have a problem with this," change your message to, "I can handle this."

Looking for Approval and Acceptance

Another thought that affects your feeling of self worth is the belief that you need the acceptance and approval of others. Self-esteem is about respecting and accepting one's self just as you are. Looking at one's talents and strengths increases self-esteem, but more often, we focus on what we have been told are our shortcomings. For example, I have a client who is unhappy in his current job. He wants to take a risk and invest in a business. Fear keeps getting in the way. When I asked him what messages he is hearing that are holding him back, he thought awhile and then shared that a junior high school teacher was very critical of him. He still hears that teacher's judgmental comments when he wants to take a risk. I suggested he write a letter to the teacher and get his feelings out—and then destroy the letter. He wrote the letter, then sent me an e-mail saying that he couldn't believe how hard it was to put it in the shredder. Part of him wanted to keep it; part of him actually wanted to mail it. He eventually shredded it and he finally felt free from the negative thoughts that held him back for over twenty years.

To attract success and raise our self-esteem, we must focus on what is special about us. We all have unique abilities, strengths, and interests, but we often lose sight of them. My work with clients involves developing personal magnetism, so they can attract what they want in life. That magnetism starts from within. When I work with clients to maximize their strengths, we look at what is fun for them. They tell me they love to play the piano, take photographs, play tennis, and lots of other things that bring them joy. When I ask if they actually do those things, they tell me they're too busy. Often clients eliminate activities that give them pleasure because they think they don't have time. But when they're doing something they enjoy, they feel more attractive, have more energy, increased self-esteem, and more capacity for attracting what they really want in life. So, what could be more important than finding time for the things you really love to do?

Other Influences

What we do and what we think aren't the only influences on our self-esteem. There are many external influences we should consider. For example, we often surround ourselves with critical, negative people. I had a friend for many years that I loved, but I realized recently that whenever I was with her I felt drained. She did nothing for my self-esteem. I remember sharing a dream I had about wanting a house on the beach. She immediately talked about all the negatives of having a house at the ocean. Having dreams are part of high self-esteem, because we feel worthy of our dreams—worthy of a house on the beach. Her negativity was detrimental to my well being. I let the friendship go. I found a new friend who is loving and supportive and who does wonders for my self-esteem. She often tells me how special I am to her and sends me loving notes and messages. In order to increase our own self worth, we must learn to set boundaries and put ourselves in an environment that is nurturing. By raising our standards for those we choose to be with, our self-esteem will increase.

Some people say they just aren't lucky. Are the people they admire lucky or is it their energy that makes them appear to be lucky? Let's explore the principles of attraction to help answer the question. Personal magnetism—our energy—not only attracts people to us, it helps us attract everything we want in life. To develop personal magnetism, first eliminate what drains us of our energy, because attraction is all about energy. We know that people in our lives can drain energy. However, you may also be surrounded by *things* that drain you. And if you are, you are taking away energy from attracting the things you want in life. You will in fact be "unattractive." That's why it's so important to eliminate energy drains. When you have more energy, you'll have more self-esteem. Consider this. Do you have clutter in your home or office? Is your desk covered with mail? Are your closets filled with clothes you don't wear? The furniture store Ikea did a survey and 31 percent of the people said they got more satisfaction from cleaning a closet than having sex. It's a pretty funny comment, but just an example of how good it feels to have an organized closet. An organized home or office gives you energy.

In addition to physical clutter, there's mental clutter, like that to-do list that's rattling around in your head. That constant buzz of things to do drains you of energy and doesn't help your confidence either. The projects that are incomplete, the calls you want to make, the errands you have to do. This mental clutter saps your energy. Here's a good way to hold onto that energy. Every morning do a "brain dump." Write three pages about all the things going on in your head and all the things that are on your mind. By writing them down and dumping them from your brain to the paper, you'll have more energy, and that adds to your attraction.

Practice Self Care

Practicing self-care increases one's self esteem. Often we are so busy with work, family, and responsibilities, that we are last on the list when it comes to priorities. We must become selfish. When I was growing up this word always had a negative feeling about it. Being selfish was a bad thing. I now see it as taking care of self. We must learn to love and care for ourselves. By showing love and respect for ourselves we are modeling for others. As we respect ourselves we will gain respect from others. Take time for yourself. Put your self-care activities on your calendar with a heart around them. Want to take yoga, an exercise class, a writing class, piano lessons? Whatever it is that you want to do, put it on your calendar in ink. Make yourself a priority. Think about what *you* really need.

Another impact on self-esteem is how we are having our needs met. What are needs, and why are they important for self-esteem? There are physical needs that must be met for us to survive. Other needs must be met for us to survive emotionally, spiritually, and mentally. Physical needs are easy to ask for, and most often, to meet. If we are hungry or thirsty, we ask for food or water. But, what about our other needs? Needs drive us. If our needs aren't met we get irritable. We're unhappy and we're not sure why. How do you get your needs met in order to feel good about yourself? The first step is identifying your needs. Look at the following list and see which ones jump out at you: to be accepted, included, respected, appreciated, complimented, understood, heard, informed, acknowledged, flattered, esteemed, to be in control. Once you identify your needs, it is important to create a system for getting them met.

For example, I had a need to be appreciated. If I did someone a favor and they didn't show their appreciation, it bothered me. When I realized I needed to be appreciated, I was able to verbalize it and make requests. My coach suggested that I ask five people in my life if they would be willing to help me to get this need met. They were happy to support me. I asked for a note, voicemail, or e-mail message telling me that they appreciate me. I asked if they were willing to do this once a week for four to six weeks. The cards and messages came in and it was great. I'm not saying the need is completely gone, but it doesn't drive me like it used to.

The important thing is not to expect others to know what you need. Whether at work or at home, when it's appropriate, verbalize what you want. A spouse or coworker might not realize how much you need to be acknowledged, respected, or complimented. Be specific. Also, don't feel that if you have to ask for it, it doesn't count. That's not true. Asking to have your needs met does not make it less effective. Don't hesitate to ask for what makes you happy. Remember needs are like food and water. They are basic conditions that must be met for us to be happy and to have high self-esteem.

If you want to make positive changes in your life, you must create good choices. So often, we don't even think about how many choices we make. What time to get up, what to wear, what to eat for breakfast are all choices that we make without thinking too much about them. Do you choose to take care of your health and exercise regularly? Do you choose to enjoy your work every day? Do you choose to have a positive attitude every day? Do you choose to speak kindly to others? Do you surround yourself with people who are caring and supportive? Do your friends build you up? The minor, daily decisions we make direct the kind of life we'll have.

I met a woman on an airplane who shared her story with me. She was a widow with six children. Her dream was to become a motivational speaker. She was raising six young children successfully and doing it with a most positive attitude. She told me a story of twin brothers. One was extremely successful and wealthy. When asked what motivated him to become so successful, he replied, "My father was an alcoholic. I had no choice." His brother couldn't hold down a job and became an alcoholic and when asked, "What caused you to become an alcoholic?" he replied, "My father was an alcoholic. I had no choice." There's a great message here: what makes us who we are is not what happens to us, but how we choose to react.

Do you consciously think about the choices you have, or do you do what you've done for years? The choices we make every day increase or decrease our self-esteem. How do you spend your free time? Are you going to worry today? Are you going to have patience today? Who are you going to spend time with today? If something happens during the day, do you ask yourself, "What do I choose to do about this?" Think about the friends you have and choices you've made. As we control our choices, we control our lives. Choose well.

When we ask ourselves what we really want, and then act to get it, our self-esteem increases. In order to have the life you want and deserve and to attract what you want, you must believe in your self worth. Having increased self-esteem is about positive self-talk, eliminating energy drains, and making the right choices. Our thoughts *do* create our reality. What are your thoughts? Are they positive? Nurturing? Loving? Create the outlook you want in your life. Think about your talents and abilities. Focus your attention on what you want to manifest. Create positive messages and tell them to yourself.

Most of us have secret desires and dreams. A high self-esteem is important for us to have the fulfilled lives we want and deserve. If we don't feel good about ourselves, we will not be able to take risks and follow the path of our dreams. Many people die having never shared their secret dreams and desires, let alone having lived them. Fear of failure holds them back. Whether it's their own negative self-talk or the old tapes from childhood, they are afraid to fail.

What is your life purpose? What is the dream in your drawer? Don't keep the dream in the drawer. Make it happen. Talk to yourself in a positive way. Change your thoughts and change your life. Treat yourself like the person you want to be and you will fulfill all of your desires and dreams.

About
Phyllis Sisenwine

Phyllis Sisenwine of Powerful Solutions, Inc. is a Professional Certified Coach (P.C.C.). A top sales producer for a major corporation for over twenty years, Phyllis shares her success strategies with her clients, coaching them to achieve exceptional growth.

In addition to being a business and personal coach, Phyllis is a professional speaker providing programs for organizations on "Attracting Success." A published author, Phyllis also has a monthly column in SBN magazine on leadership development.

Phyllis is a graduate of Coach University and was a presenter at their first international conference. Her professional affiliations include certification by the International Coach Federation, membership in Philadelphia Area Coaches Alliance, National Association of Women Business Owners, National Association of Female Executives, and she is a member of the National Speakers Association.

Phyllis has written and produced the following products:

Audio tapes: *10 Powerful Solutions for Business Success*
Powerful Networking
Become a Magnet for Success
Booklet: *101 Tips to Business Success*
Book: *Intentional Change*

To order Phyllis' tapes, booklets, or books, or to contact her, send an email to phyllis@powerfulcoaching.com, call (877) 321-8114, or visit her website at www.powerfulcoaching.com.

Self-Esteem: From the Inside Out

by Margie Summerscales Heiler

"Your vision will become clear only when you look into your heart. Who looks outside, dreams. Who looks inside, awakens."

- Carl Jung -

As I prepared to write this chapter, an organic process of self-esteem danced through my mind and into my heart. I thought of definitions, books, people I know and those I read about, as well as models and theories about self-esteem. Then, I reflected on my own process over the years, of times when I felt good about myself and of times when I didn't feel good about myself. I realized that a pivotal point for me was discovering what my purpose in life is, in addition to growing up, having a job, getting married, and having children. Thinking about self-esteem came naturally, as I enjoy introspection and embracing all the possibilities. Consequently, I reinforced my belief that self-esteem is determined by my ability to live my dreams, passions, and values.

To this end, I am no longer traveling to the places where I thought I could "pick up" self-esteem, such as from my parents, partner, children, friends, or colleagues. Self-esteem truly comes from within me as I define the ingredients, rather than allowing someone else to define who I must be, the way I must live, or what I should do. The ingredients that make up who I am and how I feel about myself include choices, intentions, and values.

The Transformational Model on page 97 supports this view. In the past, trying to fit other molds gave me a false sense of self-esteem. "Self" in self-esteem means *me*. Others can't give it to me and they can't take it away from me; it can only come from within.

In this chapter, I will present what has been true for me and countless clients I have had the distinct privilege to partner with as a coach. While I have not performed any research studies to demonstrate the statistical significance of what I propose, I have read and experienced endorsement and support for these views. The models I offer are simple, and yet profound.

Four years ago, I embarked on the current phase of my life's journey when I attended a Living Your Vision® (LYV) workshop, a program developed by Fran Fisher, Master Certified Coach and president of LYV Enterprises, Inc., in Bellevue, Washington. Living Your Vision® is a transformational process where participants identify their unique visions and purpose, clarify values, create a MasterPlan, and step into action. The workshop and the information I received have significantly changed my own life journey to enriched self-esteem and, as a result, have affected the lives of everyone I interact with and the relationships we share. The following Model for Enhanced Self-Esteem, one I developed out of what I learned at this workshop, shows that self-esteem is directly related to the principles of LYV.

FOUNDATION AND PRINCIPLES OF LIVING YOUR VISION®
MODEL FOR ENHANCED SELF-ESTEEM®

This model illustrates how self-esteem is related to the degree I am living my vision (the foundation of my essence), making choices, creating intentions, and honoring my values. Self-esteem increases exponentially as I honor the foundation and principles of living my vision. I attribute much of my success and self-esteem to the LYV process, the personal growth work I have done, and the ensuing relationships I developed with colleagues and students. The more I live by these guidelines, the more my self-esteem increases, as I feel more centered and whole. The process has enabled me to succeed in the face of today's challenges and opportunities, while maintaining a balanced and fulfilled life. This chapter describes how trusting this process has worked for me and how you can use it for yourself.

Discovering Your Unique Gifts and Talents

In the Fall of 1994, after many jobs and adventures from both heaven and hell, I discovered coaching as I now know it at the Organization Development Network Conference in Seattle. At the time, I thought I was already a coach since I had coached managers and other employees for years. However, after being introduced to this new wave of coaching, I realized that despite the fact that I was using some coaching skills in my consulting, the coaching I was exposed to at the conference was significantly different. I felt a passion surging within at the outset and decided to follow my dream by taking the next few baby steps. I now know that what I learned at the conference was just a scratch on the surface.

After the conference, I researched coaching schools for a year and participated on a national coaching board to learn more. That search led me to LYV and the full-time coaching career I enjoy today.

What I realized by finding my passion in coaching, was that discovery is the first step on the road to enhanced self-esteem. And since that discovery, my self-esteem has continued to grow. Mind you, I had many discouraging words, and found many valleys along the way to passion. Family and personal tragedies presented me with cause for both significant grief and healing. The Gremlin voices were mighty and ferocious (see Richard Carson's *Taming Your Gremlins*). Fortunately, my heightened self-esteem and belief in my abilities anchored me and kept me thriving in an ongoing transformation that has taken me beyond my wildest dreams. In a continuing fashion, it sustains me in spite of extreme personal challenges. Having found my passion, my commitment is to be engaged in this process the rest of my life.

What is Your Passion?

You, too, can experience living your dreams. To begin, my first question to you is: "What is *your* passion in life?" I am not talking about your surface craving or desire. I am asking you to go deep within yourself to your core essence and get in touch with that which makes your heart sing so loud that you can hear it. Once you find that place, you, too, can live your vision. Remember to think beyond what you currently see or imagine.

Ask yourself: "What is the feedback I have heard over and over from others? What am I really good at? What do I love doing?" For me, I narrowed it down to helping others develop the belief that they could do anything they wanted to do. In coaching terms, I refer to it as holding others big, whole, and capable.

Continuing to use my own example, I knew that making a difference in people's lives was important to me. I also view myself as a risk-taker and I have always been independent! One of the people I admired was the late Darrell Sifford, a columnist for the *Philadelphia Inquirer* and author of *What do You Think*? In an October 1983 column on Self-Esteem and Risk-Taking, he quoted California psychologist Aaron Hemsley, who said the ability to risk without debilitating anxiety stems from "the one basic thing that all risk-takers have—a high level of self-esteem. They are very confident about themselves, and they would score high if you measured them on a self-reliant scale." Coaching has allowed me to make my desires a reality, to take risks, and to make a difference.

Think about what you are drawn to right now and what or who you attract. For instance, another phenomenon about my self-discovery was how approachable I became—to the point where strangers stopped me in a store or on the street and told me things they have never told anyone. I used to say that I was wearing a "Tell Me" sign. Now, I look at it differently and welcome those interactions.

This brings me to the next set of questions for you to ask yourself: "What is it that has kept reappearing in my life as a message? Who do I admire and who are my heroes? What am I attracting into my life?" The answers to these questions will help you discover your passion.

Am I Living Inside Out?

Now, ask yourself: "Am I living inside out or outside in?" Here, I will share an abbreviated version of The Transformational Model that I mentioned earlier. This model supports the concept of living from the inside-out. The inner circle represents a person's core essence (vision), choices, intentions, and values. Circumstances of life, including people, are on the outside. What's important here is to learn how to respond rather than react to those outside circumstances. The most effective and empowering way for you to personally experience transformation and growth is from the inside out. You will have the freedom to choose, instead of being influenced by outside circumstances (environment, relationships, finances, etc). Making changes from the outside is similar to depending on the advice of others versus trusting your own answers. Your level of self-esteem depends on trusting yourself and your ability to live in alignment with your choices, intentions, and values from the inside out. We will explore choice, the power of intention, and values on the following pages.

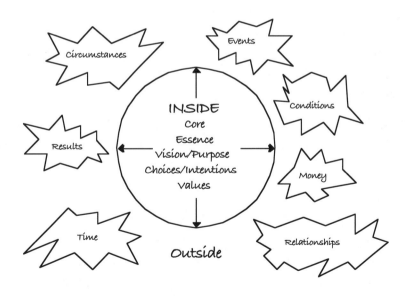

THE TRANSFORMATIONAL MODEL
© 1999 LYV Enterprises, Inc.—Permission to copy granted.

Living at Choice

For some, the word "goal" has become disempowering and does not contribute to self-esteem. As an alternative, I invite you to replace the word *goal* with the word *choice*. While setting goals is intended to be positive, the process often brings up resistance, such as pressure to perform, obligation, have to, should, etc. The word "choice" expresses a greater sense of personal freedom and self-esteem—that is, being at *choice*!

With this shift in language, you can readily move into creating a powerful structure for activities and actions for follow-through with powerful results. To reinforce the magnetic power of intention, the acronym below reflects this energizing way of being:

C = Choosing
H = Heart-centered
O = Opportunities, that are:
I = Inspiring
C = Congruent
E = Empowering
S = Specific and measurable

The intention of being at choice in your life contributes to greater acceptance, self-esteem, and increased performance. My experience has been that once people realize they can choose how they live their lives, they are more empowered and successful.

Trusting the I AM Formula

INTENTION (PURPOSE OR FOCUS) + ATTENTION (ALIGNMENT WITH FOCUS)
= MANIFESTATION (RESULT)

The formula presented above is similar to and works as well as an algebraic formula. If you are not manifesting the results you want in your life, check out your Intention and Attention, and where your energy is directed. When I was first introduced to this model, I thought it looked too simple. At the same time, I was willing to take a risk and give it a whirl. After returning home to Utah from a six-month stint on a full-time assignment in California that was supposed to be coaching and turned out to be consulting, I determined that by the end of the following year, I would be a full-time coach (Intention). Here are some of the ways I paid Attention to my Intention:

- Signing up to be on workshop teams for coaching classes in Washington at the Academy for Coach Training.
- Saying "no" to job offers and contracts for training opportunities that would drain energy and resources.
- Learning about other coaching opportunities.
- Becoming the best coach I could be.
- Enrolling coaching clients.
- Career-wise, focusing my energy on and immersing myself in coaching.
- Choosing activities that supported my intention.

By April 1, I was coaching full-time (Manifestation)!

I suggest that you state your Intention of something you desire in your life as if it were already happening—that you are living it. Ask yourself: "What is something I intend for my life right now?" As you think about that question, remember that Intention is the focus or purpose. The Intention comes from the inside out. A coach's job is to help clients clarify their Intentions and focus on them. Once the Intention is clear, write it down and you are ready for Attention. Attention is an expression of energy, alignment with the Intention, the degree of consciousness, resources, and the "how." The coach notices where the Attention is and supports the client to align with the Intention. Manifestation is the outcome, the "what."

Where in your life are you Manifesting results that you want and where are you not? What happens when your result doesn't match your Intention?

Identifying Your Values

Next, identify your top values. What are the most important values you *must* have honored in your life? Your quality of life is determined by the extent to which you are honoring those values. For example, when I looked back at a past job I held, I felt that I had sold my soul. I realized my top values were not honored and the values of the organization did not fit with some of mine. Never again will I compromise by selling out in that way.

Discovering and clarifying *your* values will provide access to your essence, self-esteem, and personal power. Aligning your actions with those values will, again, impact your quality of life. If something, someone, or a situation in your life feels uncomfortable, look at what value is not being honored. Entertain the possibility that it's a value you didn't even know you had. Recently, I had a lot of chaos and commotion in my life. I looked to my values and realized I now value peace and that did not fit amidst chaos. I recalled that years ago I thrived on chaos and commotion. Now, the discovery of honoring peace helps me pay esteem to myself and improves my quality of life.

I encourage you to embrace the values that enrich you and nourish you, ones that will bring you balance and fulfillment. To do this, you may want to complete a values clarification exercise or prioritize your top values. Clarifying values will help you in the following ways:

- Provide access to essence and personal power.
- Align your actions with your values.
- Improve your quality of life.
- Give you standards to guide conduct.
- Lend direction and focus.
- Assist with decision-making and problem-solving.
- Measure and evaluate choices.
- Promote independence and freedom.
- Support having control over your life and put you in the driver's seat of your life.
- Demonstrate credibility and authenticity.
- Help you come across to others with consistency.
- Increase self-awareness, self-acceptance, and understanding of yourself and others.
- Make you more confident.
- Give you energy.

A Values Clarification Exercise

Use the following visualization exercise and answer the questions that follow each step to start articulating your values:

- Think of and describe a time when you were feeling especially good about yourself. Identify the scenery, the people around you, the time of day, and what the weather was like. See if you can see the colors, smell the smells, get fully into the mood of that time and place. How were you feeling? Enjoy being there and feel your self-esteem rise as you experience that scene and time once again.
- * What values were being honored?
- Think of and describe a time when you were upset or angry, things were not going well, or you were having a problem.
- * What values were not being honored?
- What do you always take care of no matter what?
- * What value(s) are you honoring?
- I am most alive and feeling energized when I am honoring the following values:_____.
- * What must I have in my life and what value(s) does this honor?
- What are you known for, for example, what qualities would people use to describe you?
- * What values do these qualities represent?

A coach can help you identify your core values and offer you support structures to facilitate your personal process. A coaching relationship is a process in itself and each person's process will have different results. Once you are clear about your values, a coach will partner with you to live them.

Let me share a story about my 82-year-old mother that demonstrates how simple and yet powerful values can be. One day my mother was talking about "love" and related topics. I asked her, "What does love mean to you?" After a moment, she said, "Companionship." When I asked her what else it meant to her, she said that was all. I was astounded and realized how important companionship is to her, that it is a top value for her. This startling and yet simple revelation has changed my relationship with her in a very positive way that has increased both of our self-esteems.

What are Your Boundaries and How do You Honor Them— Without Attachment?

Having boundaries and honoring them will assist you in valuing yourself and having others value and respect you, adding to your self-esteem. In a recent conversation about boundaries, one of my clients said, "Boundaries will give me freedom." I have reveled in that statement ever since. In the past, I believed boundaries were confining and fenced me in. Today, I am keenly aware that boundaries give me freedom. For the sake of my self-esteem, I must ask for what I want and let others know what I am willing to put up with and what I am not willing to put up with. This is quite new for me and has been both challenging and rewarding. The knowledge has opened me up to being vulnerable and not taking something personally when someone says "no" or gives me feedback I'd rather not hear. Without those boundaries, however, I am not honoring my well-being and, therefore, my self-esteem.

Over the past few years, just when I think I've mastered boundaries, new opportunities appear and I'm addressing the issue all over again. Each time, my awareness and self-esteem measurements rise higher on the scale. Ask yourself, "How do I exercise boundaries in my life?"

The Results of an Ongoing Journey

Everyday I am grateful for gifts in life. I appreciate Fran Fisher and the LYV process that have contributed to my insights about myself, others, and self-esteem. Thank you also to my parents, husband, children, colleagues, clients, teachers, students, and friends for their talents and wisdom and what they have shared with me. I am privileged and completely understand that I would not be who I am today if it weren't for them. They are truly blessings and teachers for me as I continue my journey. The story I have written for myself is a beginning. In the future, more of the saga will be divulged and I intend to enjoy it fully. My future dreams include a larger retreat center at our log home in Utah, and a coaching television show. Now that I have stated those intentions, I will pay more attention to those seeds and manifest my vision.

In closing, I acknowledge my husband's enduring loyalty, support, love, encouragement, and steadiness in partnering with me on my endless journey of self-worth. Without his partnership, I could not live my dreams with the highest expression of self-esteem!

Today, I am much more comfortable with who I am and what I do. Furthermore, I have a higher self-esteem. What if you were living the life of your dreams? How would that make a difference for you? The difference it makes for you will not only impact you in a big way, it will also affect everyone in your life and the lives of those they touch. The process starts with you and you are the only one who has control over you. You are the gift with many talents.

About
Margie Summerscales Heiler

Margie Summerscales Heiler is a Master Certified Coach (M.C.C.), with a Bachelor of Arts in Psychology and a Master's in Human Organization Science. A licensed Living Your Vision® Coach, Margie is Program Director and a Senior Course Leader for LYV Enterprises, Inc., and is the Director of Training for their Academy for Coach Training in Bellevue, Washington. She also operates a successful business from her home in Utah as a Personal and Executive Coach, Coach Mentor, and Trainer.

Margie's experience includes management positions in the corporate world, as well as extensive knowledge in business and the training and organization development fields. Providing coaching for leaders, teams, and businesses, she offers a varied background along with the following certifications: Myers-Briggs, Benchmarks 360 (Center for Creative Leadership), Selling with Insight, and other models and inventories designed for communicating more effectively, exploring personality differences, and strategic planning and growth.

In Utah, Margie's office is in a rustic log home she shares with her husband, Rick. In this private, country atmosphere in the high desert surrounded by the beauty of mountains, she delivers one-on-one Living Your Vision® retreats. As a contributing author to this book, she reveals her own journey, passion, and belief in the Living Your Vision® process. She sees the tremendous and magical positive differences it has made in her own life, as well as the lives of her clients and students at the Academy.

With her passion and interest in helping people achieve their personal and professional dreams, Margie is truly a visionary leader and champion for growth. Her clients enjoy the partnership, truth, safety, trust, challenge, and fun they co-create with her in the coaching relationship.

Born in Canada, Margie has lived in California, Pennsylvania, Georgia, and Florida, and has raised four children. Today, she is living the dreams she has created and supports others in discovering and living theirs. She provides guidance to assist people in liberating their personal power so they can imagine and manifest their highest visions. As a result, her clients create intentions and make choices that lead to increased self-esteem, happiness, and improved performance and productivity.

In addition to being quoted in an article concerning career changes for *InfoWorld*, she has been interviewed numerous times about coaching and the techniques she uses. Giving presentations to a number of societies and groups contributes to her balance and fulfillment as she is committed to professional and community organizations. In her leisure time, she enjoys family and friends, her pets and horses, music, skiing, dancing, hiking, and spending time in her "sacred space."

To contact Margie, call (801) 446-0794, send an email to CoachMargie@earthlink.net, or visit www.coachtraining.com.

Dancing With the Universe: Growing Your Self-Esteem

by Judy Epstein

It is never too late to develop your inner confidence, feel content, and enjoy your "Dance with the Universe"—your journey through life. Inner confidence allows you to express your perspectives and ideas comfortably. This confidence provides you with the ability to see that other points of views are just that—a different perspective—instead of a criticism or challenge of you. Feeling content enables you to be comfortable in the here and now, as well as being open to new adventures. Nothing is needed to improve your immediate enjoyment of life, yet you readily welcome new opportunities.

Enjoying your "Dance with the Universe" means everything is happening perfectly, so you just "dance" with what is happening and discover which moves are the most harmonious and fluid. This dance is based on the belief that the Universe is benevolent and ultimately wants you to fulfill your Soul's purpose to the highest degree possible. You awaken an awareness that you are a co-creator of your life and see that the Universe is providing challenges that can become opportunities to attain a higher level of understanding. In Chinese, the character for "crisis" also means "opportunity." A perceived "crisis" challenges you beyond your everyday reactions and thus provides an "opportunity" to react differently, perhaps with a greater insight or from a broader perspective. When you're dancing in harmony with the Universe, your life progresses naturally and easily. It may look like luck, but it is a healthy level of self-esteem, experienced inwardly and mirrored back to you from the surrounding world.

At some point in our lives, many of us have experienced low self-esteem, which can manifest in a number of ways. For example, you might be shy and avoid attention, hoping no one will notice you or your perceived weaknesses. Or, you might attempt to win people over by pleasing them, despite your inner belief that you aren't really worthy of being liked. Or you might overcompensate and act boisterous and self-assured, presenting a bold exterior to hide how insecure you actually feel. Whatever the presentation, having low self-esteem leaves you hoping not to be found out as a fraud or a fake. You might even have an unspoken feeling that life is to be endured or survived.

Certain situations in the past may have contributed to low self-esteem. An incident may have left you feeling stunted or challenged. Although specific memories may be vague, a definite pattern of inner vulnerability and insecurity still lingers. With the right circumstances, you can restore and reclaim your self-esteem and its natural evolution of growth.

Self-esteem can grow by challenging and correcting old beliefs and perceptions that lead to recurring negative self-talk. Instead of doubting yourself or being riddled with insecurity, your self-confidence grows and you discover a new joy and satisfaction in life. Apprehensive tendencies about abilities, mannerisms, or even physical appearance begin to melt away and in its place, genuine self-love and acceptance begins to flourish.

To increase your self-esteem, you need to provide unfailing love and support to an inner part of yourself, usually a younger version of yourself, such as the child of your past. One way to love and support your childhood-self is to revisit and reframe the interpretations of past disappointments and gain an understanding of how these traumas can be healed and how they can serve as a blessing. Sensitively attending to the needs of your childhood-self enables you to be there for this scared little one as you so wished someone else had been there for you. You know exactly what the child (you) needed and through an experience somewhat like time-travel, you are able to provide it, helping the child feel safe, cared for, and secure. It is never too late to change the interpretation of your life's story.

Changing Interpretations

As a healer for over 20 years, I have come to understand that health and wellness emanate from the inside. "Health," or lack there-of, is the outward manifestation of what naturally flows from our inner state of being. A low level of self-esteem and its resulting effects reflect stunted inner growth in the area of self-appreciation. One of my aims as a Life Enrichment Coach is to facilitate and support the self-healing of inner experiences so that outwardly, life reflects health and wellness naturally and effortlessly. The technique I offer in this chapter is designed to lovingly heal old wounds that prevent your natural abundance of self-esteem from emerging. As a coach, I work with you as you acquire the ability to transform your life into a joyous journey filled with meaningful and enriching experiences.

Since low self-esteem is related to incidents that stunted or challenged your sense of self, it is important to revisit those moments and change your interpretations of them. Often these situations are from childhood, for that is when you learned what you know about yourself and how you perceived your place in the world. These events became defining moments in your life, though rarely with conscious recognition. Actively recalling them and recognizing the strategies you used as a young child to cope with them creates an opportunity to gain insights, to transform your perception of the incident into one that encourages and supports the growth of self-esteem.

For example, we repeatedly tell ourselves the same story about our childhood circumstances. We give ourselves reasons why we're "not worthy." We may have forgotten some stories because their content was too uncomfortable, yet we remember their message. Each time we recall these stories or their message, they become more real, painful, and indisputably believable. We make it into an irrefutable event without any other way for it to have happened or for it to mean anything else. This phenomenon contributes to our inability to change our level of self-esteem, even when we wish it to change.

That is why changing the story you tell yourself is critical to changing your level of self-esteem. Changing your story is, in essence, replaying and rewriting important moments in your personal history. For you to accept these new stories as real and possible, the material outcome of your event cannot be changed. If something bad happened to you, unfortunately you cannot rewrite the story of your life and say that it didn't happen. However, you can and must change how you *perceived* the incident. In other words, the event remains the same, yet you create and nurture a broader, more self-loving interpretation. Using compassion, love, and support for what you felt as a child, you introduce your present-day adult's insight and guidance to replay the incident and bring new meaning. This new understanding helps correct the erroneous interpretations you had as a child, and what contributed to your lack of self-worth and value.

Your new understanding might be as simple as learning that the hurtful things said in past childhood memories were more about the person saying them than they were about you, and that there was no absolute truth in them. As a young child, naïve and totally dependent on others, you believed such statements were true and then later reinforced them in your own mind. By revisiting the incident, you can change your interpretation of what really happened.

Let's use "Susan" as an example. Susan is a woman with difficulty in personal relationships. Her low self-esteem causes her to overcompensate with overly strong self-assurance. She displays a tough and hardened attitude of "I can take you or leave you," pretending that she has everything together and is managing fine on her own. Susan's behavior is her way of coping and covering up her feelings of vulnerability in relationships. At some level, she feels that people will inevitably hurt her because she isn't worthy of their friendship. She might as well reject them first and save herself from the pain. As she ages, this stance interferes with her ability to have intimate relationships, which she now desires. Susan doesn't know what to do to change, though she realizes that she must somehow remedy how she feels about herself.

To change her behavior, Susan must first come to understand her present reactions and how she came to rely on them. She must recognize that there is a pattern to her reactions and the situations that attract them. Finding ourselves faced with similar challenges over and over again is no fluke. Repetition is one way the Universe gets our attention. If we miss the message, the situations tend to be more dramatic and intense. Eventually, we might ask, "What is going on here?" Although initially the question is rhetorical, another part of us eventually hears the whisper from the Universe, that there is no coincidence here. Then that small part of us begins to awaken and watch, witnessing a definite connection and pattern to such circumstances.

Uncovering the significance of these connections on your own requires astute awareness, and can be augmented with the help of a coach. Like coming to a section of the trail that isn't well marked, you have to closely observe signs revealing where the trail goes. Sometimes this requires that you backtrack to make sure you didn't misread the path and miss a turn. With feelings, this astute awareness takes on the form of self-inquiry: "What am I really feeling? Is that an emotional feeling or a judgement? If it is a judgment, what is the hidden emotion behind it? What am I afraid of? What are my secret fears about this?"

In this example, Susan has already come to the realization that there is a pattern, but hasn't explored the dynamics any further. Later, when she is in a crowded department store, she finds herself disgusted with all the helpless shoppers around her. She silently thinks, "What is wrong with you people? Why don't you get out of my way and get a life!" However, this time a part of her is aware and witnessing what she is thinking, and recognizes this is a common reaction of hers. She is acting as though others are just in her way and offer no value to her whatsoever.

On her way home, she explores her feelings more closely and discovers that her reaction was an emotional response. "To what," she asks herself. "What am I afraid of?" After a moment of soul-searching, she finds her answer. "I'm afraid of not getting what I want." Surprised by her honesty, she explores the inquiry further, "What are my secret fears about this?" To her amazement, she hears the answer: "I always have to fight for everything I want. No one is going to help me so I have to find a way to get it on my own."

In this example, we see that the first step for Susan is awareness. The next step is a willingness to understand the origin of her feelings. From this place of inner honesty, she can begin to see how she uses her anger and disgust with others to distance herself from her own deeper feelings. She understands that her detachment is how she avoids her real feelings toward herself and to others. She also sees that her cynical attitude encourages this pattern to continue; it keeps her distant. With this new insight, she begins to be more aware of underlying emotions every time she catches herself being cynical.

In Susan's "Dance with the Universe," this awareness provides opportunities for her to recognize and address her underlying issues of intimacy with herself and others. As she perceives these opportunities and gracefully responds to them, she begins to "dance" her way through life. Catching on to the "Dance," the Universe sends its very own private "wink" that no one else can see. When you learn to recognize it amidst the everyday events of your life, this "wink" from the Universe reassures you that you are definitely on the right path. Unexpected incidents arise yet now they become new dance moves from the Universe. As you catch on, your responses to these "moves" become more fluid and graceful; you are enjoying and mastering your "Dance with the Universe."

To restore and reclaim a greater level of self-esteem, Susan's next step is to explore childhood memories for clues of when she might have first felt the feeling that "no one is going to help me." She can't remember all of the details, but she clearly recalls her first day of preschool. In a corner of the playground, away from any adults who might help or protect her, some classmates surrounded her, making fun of how she was dressed. Frightened, she wished for her mother's protection, and silently endured their taunts. When she shared her anxiety about going back to preschool with her mother later that night, her mother dismissed her fear, telling her that the other kids didn't mean anything by it, and that things would get better. The next day, the other kids picked on her again. However, this time Susan felt too ashamed to tell her mother. "They must pick on me because I'm not as good as they are," she thinks to herself. "What they are telling me is true—my clothes do look funny on me because I'm funny looking."

Years later, the stories in her mind still play and the same vulnerable feeling remains. However, now she has learned that if she is tough and bullies someone else, she won't be the scapegoat nearly as much. She has developed her "you can't touch me" attitude as a response.

Rewriting the Story

Having recalled the incident that sowed the seeds of her current behavior, Susan can now begin to rewrite the story and heal the misinterpretations. To do so she must revisit them. Almost as if she is able to travel back to her past, Susan's present-day, compassionate self talks with the little girl of her childhood. Her adult self helps the little girl feel safe and kindly guides her toward new insights, transforming the event into more of a learning situation, with much less fear and pain.

To have this conversation between the little girl of her past and her present-day adult, Susan must play both roles, giving a different voice and mannerism to each part. One way she may do this is to use two chairs, one for her to sit in when she is the little girl and the other for her to sit in when she is the loving adult. Sitting in different chairs helps her to take on different perspectives and allows that perspective to develop and speak uninterrupted until the other's response is sought. For Susan, actually changing positions clarifies which part of herself—little girl or adult—is speaking.

At first, this process of dialogue feels awkward for Susan. She is not sure what to say in either role and feels a little intimidated. However, she soon realizes that she knows each role intimately, for they are both her. Susan therefore quiets herself and tunes in. She begins to remember how she felt and what she needed when she was the little girl. She remembers this particular story for a specific reason—to heal the pain of it. Susan realizes that she is more comfortable giving to others, so she decides to pretend she is responding to her best friend or her best friend's little girl if they had the same feelings that she had in childhood. In this way she naturally accesses the loving and helpful present-day adult and applies it to herself by listening closely to what she says. The wisdom comes through her and she stays cognizant of what she says so she can absorb it for herself.

Let's listen in on the dialogue as Susan plays out the different roles of herself—the adult and her little girl:

"Honey, come sit down with me. I want to talk with you," adult Susan says as she motions to the chair sitting across from her.

The little girl sits down in the chair as she tentatively responds, "Okay."

"You know, you might not believe this, but I saw what happened to you in preschool," Susan begins.

The child remains silent, but stares at Susan in disbelief. As the little girl fidgets with her feet, Susan continues, "I want you to know that you did nothing wrong. I saw how frightened and alone you felt."

"Then why didn't you help me!" the girl replies with a sniffle.

"Oh, honey, I wanted to. I don't want you to hurt like that. But you know what? You learned something important from this today."

The child answers resentfully, "No, I didn't. If you don't want me to hurt, then why didn't you stop them?"

Gently, Susan replies, "I didn't say you learned something fun, just something important. After a long pause, she asked, "Aren't you curious to know what?"

"Kinda," the child tentatively whispers.

"Those children were mean to you today. They said things that weren't nice and weren't true. Your clothes don't look silly on you and you aren't funny looking. In fact, you have a special beauty inside of you and when you are happy, it shines through so everyone can see it."

"But I wasn't happy," the little girl pouts.

"I know that, dear. And I know you weren't expecting them to be mean to you."

The little girl eagerly agrees, "I wasn't. I just wanted to make friends at school. Why did they hate me?"

"Oh, honey, I don't think they hated you. I think that they may have been scared, too," she tenderly explains.

With a vigorous shaking of her head, the little girl emphatically says, "Nuh-uh."

"You know, some people pick on others when they feel scared or angry. They cover up their own feelings by making someone else feel scared. But really, they might be just as frightened as you inside. Otherwise they wouldn't need to pick on anyone."

Confused, the little girl confesses, "I don't understand."

"I know, it doesn't make sense, does it? Well, you never really know what is going on for someone else. They may look and act happy, but for all we know they might not be. They might not have a nice home where they feel safe. Maybe their parents aren't home to look after them or when they are, there is fighting going on that is very frightening to them. Or maybe they have an older brother or sister or a neighbor who picks on them constantly, and they don't have anyone to talk to like you have right now with me. We just don't know for sure what is going on with someone else. The important thing to learn is that just because someone says something mean about you doesn't mean it's true. And just because they are mean to you doesn't mean that the problem is *you*. Do you understand what I'm saying?" Susan asks.

"People are mean when they are hurting?" the little girl asked incredulously.

"Yes, sometimes they are. And it says more about them than it does you!"

"So, I didn't do anything wrong for them to be mean to me?" she asks.

Susan answers, "Not from what I saw, dear."

With a sigh of relief, the little girl says, "Oh." After a thoughtful minute, she adds, "But what happens when they pick on me tomorrow?"

Realizing the opportune time to help and guide her younger self, Susan gently explains, "Here's the thing. Remember I told you that I saw everything that happened today and you thought you were all alone? Well, I want you to remember that I'm always with you even though you may not see me. I know what you are feeling. I'm like your special secret friend. And whenever you want to talk with me, just let me know and we'll talk like this again."

"Okay!" Then after another pause, she inquires, "But you aren't going to stop them from picking on me, are you?"

"That's right, dear. You're going to have to learn how to handle that on your own. But I can tell you another secret. When you feel good about yourself and you know I'm always watching you and loving you, other people won't be able to hurt your feelings so easily. You'll learn that they don't know who you really are. They may say untrue or mean things but their actions say more about them than it does about you."

The little girl looks into Susan's eyes as she listens. She believes this adult Susan and feels safe knowing she is there with her.

"You see, I know you better than anyone in the whole world," Susan continues. "I was you when I was a little girl. And now I'm an adult that can be with you whenever you need me. You see, I didn't have someone like me when I was a little girl and I remember how scared and alone I felt at times. That is why I'm here for *you*! I'm going to help you feel safe and loved and happy inside. And then you will help me!"

"I will?" asked the girl with surprise. "How?"

"Because you'll grow up feeling better about yourself and you'll grow more and more confident, because I'll be there to help you. And soon, you'll grow up to be me! And then we both will feel better about ourselves. We'll both feel safe and loved and happy inside. What do you think about that?"

"That's neat. I like that you are here with me. I like you! Will you be my best friend?"

"Of course, dear", Susan replies lovingly, "I love you very much. And I'll be with you the rest of your life, I promise. Always remember that."

The little girl is delighted. She already feels prepared to go to preschool and isn't so afraid anymore. She now has a secret friend and that makes all the difference to her.

Susan's inner childhood-self now has a whole new understanding of her first day at preschool. In fact, she now has a best friend to help her and love her…always! The external outcome of her situation didn't change, yet because of her talk with the present-day adult, the internal has. Now when Susan's inner little girl encounters other painful experiences, she can talk with her new best friend—her loving present-day adult—like she did today. Susan further reassures her younger self that she will be there to help with all challenges. She will be there to make sense of the world around her. And if she doesn't know what to say, she promises that she will find help through her present-day adult contacts and resources, and come back later to share what she learns.

This builds an even closer and stronger bond between them. The little girl learns that she really isn't alone anymore and that she really *is* cared for and loved. More importantly, this exercise also teaches the present-day Susan about loving all of herself much more completely and inclusively. With this new improved self-love comes more inner confidence and happiness. Susan's present-day life becomes much more safe and comfortable and she experiences more joy and satisfaction with herself and others. Relationships with others soon blossom naturally because being honest, fully present, and compassionate with herself allows her to connect with others in an equal manner. She no longer needs the pretense of acting tough or being untouchable. Healing and transformation is occurring from the inside and radiating outward.

Cultivating Everyday Awareness

Susan's dialogue illustrates transforming and healing of misinterpretations of painful childhood experiences. To cultivate everyday awareness, this same process is modified to address present-day situations, when the inner child is acting out and controlling behavior. For example, Susan might tend to have a well-ingrained automatic response to make insulting comments in response to anger based on old tapes from her past. Susan now needs to work on her present-day reactions based on past misinterpretations. She needs to become conscious of her reactions and realize that they are based on the old information.

Susan must now be watchful for when her inner little girl is acting out. A good clue that this is happening is when strong, disproportionate feelings surface. These almost uncontrollable reactions allow Susan to recognize the inner child's fears, and by addressing them immediately, enables Susan to reassert herself as the care-taking adult, so the child doesn't try to handle the situation on her own. Rather than just trying to silence or obliterate the inner child, Susan can talk with her inner child in a similar type of dialogue as in the example above, validating her feelings and helping her see the situation in a new way. Since the inner child's reaction is occurring in the present, Susan informs her inner child that she, as the loving, present-day adult, will handle the situation.

The final challenge Susan now faces is staying cognizant of when her little girl is responding to fears, and building her inner child's trust that she as an adult is always around to help. The inner child begins to trust that the adult is there to take care of her and lets the adult handle these situations; fears melt away and are healed.

The amazing thing about this invented dialoguing with your child-self is that it really does change the present dynamics. The replay and rewrite of your story manifests real changes in the present, creating dramatic and uplifting results. You introduce and reinforce new understanding that things in your life happened the way they were supposed to, even if it is only now that their meaning becomes clear and nurturing. This changes the focus from the outcome of situations to the process of life. A shift begins to occur; the little child from your past begins to perceive life through your helpful eyes and feels safe, loved, and no longer alone. In both your inner child and your present-day adult, your self-esteem grows in leaps and bounds and life reflects this grace and confidence back to you.

The coaching skills I employ to facilitate this process involve hearing and gently eliciting your core feelings, identifying meaningful connections to repetitive patterns of reaction, and creatively designing exercises that reconstruct and introduce much needed love and guidance. This method heals and transforms the painful messages you internalized early on and restores your self-confidence and innate joy. We change the old context of your interpretations by replaying and rewriting the original incident and rebuild new ones by modifying your interpretations of them in ways that acknowledge and celebrate who you *really* are by divine right! This frees you from past patterns and liberates you to blossom into your full potential, supported and encouraged as you journey through the rest of your life.

As one client expressed her experience, "When I began I had all the fears and patterns of my past plaguing me. That is no longer the case—now I see challenge and opportunity for growth where before I saw insecurity and anxiety. Now I am free to be whoever I want to become; before I had no idea who I was and let others decide for me. Now I am motivated by my desire to expand myself—to reach higher and aspire for a greater purpose; before I was disoriented and unsure of my role. I am on a great new adventure into my future. I create new pathways, new connections—I face my future with an open heart and an open mind. Everywhere I turn, I find myself surrounded by friends and supporters—people who offer to help me, who are encouraging me to move forward and take risks. I am no longer alone, living in a state of self-imposed isolation. I have traveled far though have never really gone anywhere. I am who I am supposed to be—who I am destined to be. I have found my mind and my heart and can hear the song of my soul. I walk down a different street. There are no limits."

May you, too, hear the song of your soul and dance joyously with the Universe.

About
Judy Epstein

Judy Epstein, RN, BSN, LMT, NCTMB, CHTP, CNMT, PCC, works with individuals who desire a more rewarding, meaningful, and organized life. Her Life Enrichment Coaching brings balance, meaning, and joy into every aspect of her client's life, promoting their whole-being vitality and productivity. She has honed these skills through her extensive professional experiences as a healer.

Growing up in a family of healthcare providers, Judy seemed destined to be a healer. Throughout her personal life she witnessed differing approaches to healing and healthcare with a father who was a general surgeon and a mother who was a Master's prepared public health nurse and a recognized authority on rural health care. Her older brother pursued healing as a chiropractor, and her older sister worked as a neonatal intensive care nurse and later as an assistant director of respiratory research for a prominent drug company. In following her own calling, Judy created a synergistic holistic healing approach and philosophy using all of her training and life experience.

Her training in energetic healing work heightened and cultivated her skills in restoring balance and health for clients whose energy became restricted or blocked. Seeing how energy stagnates when a person is not living a harmonious life consistent with their inner values and how this stagnation leads to discomfort or disease, Judy expanded her role as teacher/healer in 1996 to include the profession of Coaching. Judy established herself as a Life Enrichment Coach, gaining Professional Certified Coach status from the International Coach Federation in 1999.

She lives in both Tucson, Arizona and in the nearby mountain community of Mt. Lemmon with her husband and two Australian Shepherds. She enjoys a balanced and nourishing life of work, play, and creative endeavors. Her professional activities include Life

Enrichment Coaching, several modalities of healing bodywork, lecturing and presenting self-help workshops at Canyon Ranch Health Resort, doctors' offices, and some public settings. Judy also markets her self-designed Strap-On Cool Packs, artistic abstract photographs of nature, and is a major distributor of the Shiatsu Hoop, a self-massage tool.

In the near future, Judy plans to write a book presenting examples of "Dancing with the Universe" and publicize the information from her self-help workshops that teaches how to rehabilitate old injuries and prevent the aches and pains associated with aging.

To order any of her products, or to contact Judy, call (520) 760-2802, send an email to nRichLife@aol.com, or visit her website at www.LifeEnrichmentCoach.com.

It's All About Me!
Who Else Would My Life Be About?

by Rachelle Disbennett-Lee

Although self-esteem is something that has been studied for 100 years, it is amazing how little most people know about the subject or understand its importance. According to Dr. Matthew McKay and Patrick Fanning in the book *Self-Esteem*, "Self-esteem is essential for psychological survival. It is an emotional sine qua non. Without some measure of self-worth, life can be enormously painful, with many basic needs going unmet." Self-esteem isn't something that we are born with, it is something we develop as we grow, as our concept of who we are develops.

Unfortunately, many of us received messages as we were growing up that made our concept of who we are and the development of high self-esteem a challenge. We were told not to "blow our own horn" or "not to get too full of ourselves." We were taught that bragging wasn't a good thing and that we should be modest and humble. For many of us, that translated into not shining our light too bright by holding back our true brilliance.

Self-esteem may seem like a simple concept, but I find many people struggle with the idea. The word esteem simply means to value something or someone; to think something or someone is important. For example, you may have a person you admire, which means you hold that person in high esteem. A special trophy for the Most Valuable Player (MVP) of a team is often called "an esteemed trophy." What this means is that the trophy is a symbol for accomplishing something that is important. The word "self" means "you." When the two words are put together, they simply mean "valuable you." To have self-esteem means that you value yourself and know how important you are. Self-esteem is the lens in which you see yourself and your accomplishments.

Most of the people I coach have self-esteem issues. Unfortunately, this doesn't seem to be too unusual. One of the saddest things I have ever read was an article in <u>Parade Magazine</u> about the Duchess of York, Sarah Ferguson. The article was an interview given by the Duchess about how she pulled herself out of debt, a very public divorce, and how she has struggled with weight and self-esteem issues most of her life. Although successful by most measures, she confessed in the article that she still does not love herself, although she is working on it. When I read this, I realized that self-esteem doesn't have to do with money or fame; it has to do with how we feel about ourselves at a core level.

Most of my clients do not hire me to help them with self-esteem, but all of them struggle with some lack of it. Many have issues with boundaries, or how other people treat them. The ability to set boundaries is one of the basic components of creating strong self-esteem. People with weak boundaries allow others to mistreat them, thus leading to a spiraling down of self-esteem. In his book, *A Woman's Self-Esteem: Stories of Struggle, Stories of Triumph*, Nathaniel Branden points out that when we have a high level of self-esteem, we tend to treat others well and to require that they treat us well also. We are clear about our boundaries and what is and is not acceptable treatment from others. We refuse to accept ill treatment and we identify with love and joy, not suffering. We feel worthy of love, happiness, and success in all areas of our lives.

The first step in coaching someone on boundary issues is to help them to understand that they deserve better and to have them start treating themselves better. As Rich Hatch, the first "Survivor" from the reality television show says, "Make your own happiness your top priority. If you don't, nobody else will." Most people with low self-esteem put themselves last and treat themselves poorly. The trick to building strong self-esteem is to take baby steps. Begin doing small things, like creating habits of positive self-talk and performing acts of self-care. In her book *Celebrate You: Building Your Self-Esteem,* Julie Tallard Johnson says it very simply, "Positive self-esteem is rooted in a deep acceptance of yourself, despite your shortcomings, mistakes, or disabilities. It includes accepting responsibility for your own well-being and taking full charge of your life. Your primary responsibility in life is your own development and well-being." Once my clients begin to take better care of themselves, they can then start letting others know how they can and cannot be treated. This is usually a difficult step and one that needs to be taken slowly. However, my clients find the results well worth it.

One client that I have coached for several years had very low self-esteem in the beginning of our coaching relationship. She was burdened with all the responsibility of the family, her husband and children were rude to her, and her home was in chaos. One of the first assignments I gave her was to simply take fifteen minutes a day for herself. She struggled with the assignment at first. Once she was comfortable with that, she created more space and time in her life for herself and began to take better care of herself. Slowly over time she developed self respect and began to tell her friends and family "no" when they would make demands on her time that were out of line. She started letting people know what they could and could not do around her and she started setting boundaries. She refused to let her family members treat her with disrespect. She lost many of her friends in the process. Even her family was put off at first. Now that the family has become accustomed to the new her, they are respectful and comment that the family actually functions more smoothly now that she is not doing everything and has everyone chipping in. She has made new friends and tells me she is happier than she has ever been.

One of the outcomes of developing a strong self-esteem and setting clear boundaries is that some people will self-select out of our lives. They simply will not be able to adjust to the changes we are making. We also might elect to eliminate people from our lives that no longer fit our new concept of ourselves. This can be difficult at first. I have had several clients get very concerned about this and feel like they were going to lose all their friends. And some do. But what happens as we raise our standards of how we treat ourselves and create strong healthy boundaries? We attract people into our lives that are willing to treat us with respect and be the type of friends that we deserve. According to Branden, "The higher our self-esteem, the more disposed we are to form nourishing, rather than toxic relationships. This is because like is drawn to like, and health is attracted to health. Vitality and expansiveness in others are naturally more appealing to personas of good self-esteem than are emptiness and dependency. Self-confident women and men are naturally drawn to one another. Alas, insecure women and men are also drawn to one another, and form destructive relationships."

I too, have experienced the loss of friends as I create stronger boundaries and develop higher levels of self-esteem. When I first became a coach, Thomas Leonard, the founder of Coach University, remarked in a class he taught, that in the first year of coaching I should expect that my rolodex would completely change. He said that the people I knew at that moment would not be the people I would know a year from then. I thought he was nuts. After all, he was talking about my close friends and colleagues. However, as I grew and developed, my old friends dropped away and new friendships began. This is a natural process as we develop into the people that we want to be. Learning to love ourselves and creating higher levels of self-esteem means that we can no longer tolerate having people in our lives that do not respect us and treat us well. This is much like the alcoholic that discovers once they stop drinking that they can no longer hang around their drinking buddies because of the risk that they might be pulled back into the same situation. Learning to love ourselves while creating higher levels of self-esteem means that we change from the inside out, and we can no longer be with people or in situations that do not positively support us.

In my mid-thirties, I began to realize that being unique was a good thing, and that I wasn't strange. I was simply different than most of the people I knew. I began to learn that my differences were what made me uniquely me. When I became a coach in 1996, I began to experience the bliss that being me brought and what it felt like to put me first in my life. I began to build a personal foundation that included strong boundaries and high standards for me, the cornerstones of a strong self-esteem. Loving yourself and believing in your worth is the firmest possible foundation upon which to build your life.

As my 40th birthday approached, I decided to throw myself a party to be remembered by all who attended. I was always the person that gave parties for others, arranging at least one surprise birthday party for each member of my family. My husband readily admits that his birthday never amounted to much until he met me.

Although I have always been the one to provide parties for friends and family, I had not had a birthday party since I was six. At some point, I began to resent giving parties for everyone else, and not having one for myself. My husband volunteered to organize my 40th, but I knew this was something I had to do for myself. When it comes to building self-esteem, it is an inside do-it-yourself job.

As I began to plan my party, I shared the details with friends and colleagues. People began to say, "Well that sounds like it is all about you." I was confused by this comment because I couldn't figure out who else my party would be about, and thus the theme "It's all about me" arose.

I decided to take the theme to extreme. I had the party of all parties. Barbie (the doll) had turned 40 the year before and I loved the dress that she wore to celebrate her "Anniversary" so much that I had a local seamstress make the dress for me. I had 200 gold and purple balloons, gorgeous flower centerpieces, a box of Godiva chocolate for each guest, and goodie bags with pins that read "It's all about me." I had live music, a massage therapist giving chair massages, a woman twisting balloons into animals, an open bar, and a castle cake. The party was truly an event.

As luck would have it, there was a snow-storm the night of my party. And still, 120 of my close friends showed up. As people arrived, they literally gasped at how beautiful the room and my gorgeous Barbie dress was. The party got under way, the appetizers were cleared, and we sat to have dinner. My friend, Kathryn Severns, who had helped pull everything together, rushed over and said I needed to explain what was going on. The guests were confused. So, I went up to the podium, as I did many times that evening, and said, "All eyes on me." Then I announced that we were having cheesecake as the first course for our dinner because it was my birthday and I could do whatever I wanted. We then proceeded to have a five-course dinner, including cake and ice cream, followed by a movie of my life, and a game that was "All about me" with t-shirt prizes that said, "It's all about me."

To say the party was a success would be an understatement. It truly was one of the best times of my life. What I found interesting was that people told me that they could never have done anything like that. They could never be so brave and make themselves the center of attention. This made me wonder: if we are not the center of attention of our lives, who is? And if we can't celebrate the moments of our lives, who will? We can't wait for others to do it for us. If we are going to have strong self-esteem, we must be willing to step out and create our own special moments. We need to be in charge of our own life.

Having my outrageous 40th birthday party was a major step for me in claiming my personal power, and accepting and celebrating who I am. The party was my way of announcing that I was proud to be 40 and proud to be me. The party was a turning point for me in embracing and loving myself.

Creating high levels of self-esteem doesn't mean we become self-absorbed narcissists. Actually just the opposite happens. As we begin to develop a loving relationship with ourselves, we create more space in our lives for others. When we treat ourselves well and develop a high level of self-esteem, we naturally want to be with others and share our love of life. We give from a place of caring and gratitude, not one of should, must, and have to. We no longer are the suffering martyr. We give from a place of abundance. When we are giving from a place of low self-esteem, we can become drained, resentful, and angry. Creating high levels of self-esteem is an act of love that not only affects our lives, it positively affects the lives of the other people in our life.

It's all about me. Who else would my life be about? If your life isn't about you, then it is time to ask yourself, "Why?"

About
Rachelle Disbennett-Lee

Coach Rachelle is an international coach with 17 years of corporate management experience in the telecommunication industry. Rachelle is certified as a Professional Certified Coach (PCC) by the International Coach Federation and has been coaching since 1996.

Rachelle has a Master's degree in Management from Regis University and is a part-time faculty member at the University of Phoenix, Denver Campus. She is working toward a Doctorate degree at Walden University in Applied Management and Decision Sciences with a specialization in Business Coaching.

Rachelle is a graduate of Coach University, the senior trainer at the International Coach Academy, has taught coaching classes at Colorado Free University for five years, and is Co-Founder of the Denver Coach Federation.

Rachelle is a published writer and is often quoted as an expert in coaching, most recently in the <u>Los Angeles Times</u>. Rachelle is the publisher of "365 Days of Coaching," an award winning e-zine that is delivered to your e-mail each morning with wisdom, motivation, and inspiration. To become a member subscriber, which includes full use of the subscriber only area on the website, visit the www.365daysofcoaching.com website.

To contact Rachelle, call (303) 617-6196, send an email to rachelle@coachlee.com, or visit her website at www.coachlee.com.

Esteemed Choices of the Financially Free

by Loral Langemeier

What occurs first, financial freedom resulting in a healthy self-esteem, or a healthy self-esteem that allows one to base their actions in ways to achieve financial freedom? As a result of coaching thousands of people for the past 12 years, I am going to suggest that the latter is true. A person with high self-esteem, confidence, and knowledge commits themselves to financial freedom. A person with low self-esteem, hesitation, and uncertainty submits themselves to financial frenzy.

Self-esteem is driven from the vision of self. To have a compelling vision of self requires time, energy, and purposeful focus on one's personal process and learning. This chapter is dedicated to those who have been seeking financial peace of mind. The peace will come from a vision of self that integrates the wealth available to you. Most people sabotage themselves by not doing the work on their self-esteem—self-vision, self-concept, who they are being. The scale continuum ranges from the very positive—one who excels, performs at a high pace, and has a positive sense—to the other extreme ranging from the very negative, feelings of worthlessness, and uncertainty. We know that life is the result of all the choices we have made in the past. Unless we consciously shift our vision of self, we will continue to get the same results.

In this chapter, I will share what I see as *choices* to financial freedom. I want to share the capacity that it takes to get there and stay there. Although the information is available to all, I specifically want women to be encouraged to stand in power and choice in their financial life. Take personal responsibility and make life what you deserve. Financial freedom *is* available to everyone. Make the choice now to begin the journey.

Esteemed Choices of the Financially Free

Creating wealth and freedom is available to everyone. My hope is that people take their space and know they deserve it. Unfortunately, in our society many people learn from an early age that money is bad, dirty, only for evil people, and that we must work hard for it. I believe that money, sex, and God are the most important subjects for children to learn about, and the three subjects least talked about in school.

Take a moment and reflect on the following thought: "Money is..." What did you think about? Some people say money is energy, spirit, fun, easy, creative, and so on. That's what most people "want" money to be. The truth is that when most people think about money, they think that money is hard, you have to work for it, it only comes monthly, rich people are bad, and, well, you get the idea. Clients who have low self-esteem and can not see themselves as "rich," "free," and financially confident, consistently reinforce their truth that they are not deserving of money. The truth is seen in action. I can look at someone's calendar and checkbook and know what they are committed to.

Exercise: Do a three-month review of your calendar and checkbook. Examine your check register for what was spent, how much, to whom, etc. This will take time! Look for themes (miscellaneous shopping, clothes, groceries, etc.) and patterns of spending time and money. Are your spending and time commitments getting the results you want?

Results, or the lack of them, are why most people seek financial and business coaching. Results are driven by actions, actions are driven by language, and language is driven by thought. Let's reverse that last statement. Your *thoughts* about yourself (self-esteem) affect how you talk to yourself and others (language) and reflect your beliefs. Do you believe that you are worthy enough to be financially secure? Does your language reflect that belief? If so, what actions do you take to ensure that security? On the other hand, if you have a low self-esteem, your thoughts will very likely steer you away from acquiring a language around actions that will ensure your financial well being. And you will remain with both low self-esteem, and little or no financial security.

R-A-L-T™: RESULTS = ACTION + LANGUAGE + THINKING

Your thinking has the most impact on the results you have in your life. Don't like your results? Change your thinking!

Getting Started: Purpose and Vision

Your first choice is to be clear about your purpose and to create a vision. *Put your purpose and vision in writing,* with a time frame and specific accountabilities.

Most people who are lacking financially do not have a compelling vision of self or a clear idea of the direction they should take to get where they want to be. Too many people are committed to current reality and thus spin around in circles because there is no "point A" and "point B." Motivation occurs when the vision of what you want (B) is clearly more compelling than current reality (A). This "motivation gap" between reality and vision is powerful. Once motivated, the next requirement is commitment. You must be committed to "a better place," or the reality will remain, and the vision will be just that—a vision.

Exercise: What is the better place for you? What are you passionate about? Clearly articulate and write out your personal vision statement? (This is a crucial assignment to begin raising your self-esteem/vision of self.)

Review Current Financial Situation

The second choice is to take stock of your current financial situation. Once this is in place, create a plan that leads to your vision. You can't decide where to go until you know where you are.

FINANCIAL STATEMENTS

Let's look at the basic vocabulary for creating a financial statement. There are two primary personal financial statements.

The first is your **Balance Sheet:** your **assets** and your **liabilities**. This is simply what **you own (assets)** and what **you owe (liabilities).** Subtract your debt or liabilities from your assets and you get your **net worth.** Your net worth is rarely what you think. This is an ever-changing reflection of how well you are playing the money game. Know what you're worth! *Net worth = assets – liabilities.*

The second financial statement is an **Income Statement**, your monthly **income** and **expenses**. If this is done for a business, it is called a **profit and loss** statement. This is a reflection of how much money you make and how much you spend.

If you subtract expenses from income, you get the **disposable income** or **cash flow.** Most people spend their extra monthly cash flow on personal, immediate gratification. Disposable income is the money that you could spend on investment. **Cash flow =**

income - expenses. Knowing where your money comes from and how much you have is crucial. Equally important is to know where it goes. With the personal financial statement, you will have a clear picture of current reality.

Exercise: Fill out your personal financial statement and notice what it is showing you. What is your net worth? What is your monthly cash flow? What does this say about you and your life? What do you want to change?

Examine Beliefs

The third choice for getting started is to look deeply at your beliefs. What we think about is what we create. You get what you expect. Our mind is composed of our conscious and subconscious mind. This is where all of our thoughts are impressed. When we are children, our subconscious mind is like an open funnel, and all that goes in will soon be the backdrop for our decision-making. For example, if you grew up in a household with parents who consistently said, "We can't afford it, we live paycheck to paycheck, you have to work hard for your money," your subconscious will hold on to those thoughts.

So for instance, if you would win a million-dollar lottery, the conscious mind will perceive the million bucks coming in and get all excited—yeah, I won! Immediately, the conscious mind checks in with the subconscious mind and asks, "Have you seen anything like this before?" If your subconscious belief is that "I live paycheck to paycheck," guess what? Your subconscious mind will create decisions and actions to ensure that you do. A million dollars may take a while to spend, yet what we know about millionaire lottery winners is that only 2 % ever retain their winnings. You must make the *choice* to know what you think. Become aware of your self-talk.

Exercise: Listen and record your self-talk for one week. At the end of each day, reflect on your thoughts and record them. Look for patterns and time spent on certain areas of thought.

Once you encounter negative thinking, *choose to change it* through this exercise:

Old Belief / Thought	**New Positive, Present Affirmation**
I live paycheck to paycheck.	Money is always available.
Money is hard to get.	Money flows freely and easily.

Make a list and then 50 + times per day for one month reaffirm your new positive, present affirmation of thought. Even if it feels strange, stay with it. Focus on your vision of what you want!

Creating Your Financial Plan

Just like you have a plan for your health, your vacation schedule, your schooling, *you must have a plan for your finances*—and spend time supporting that plan. Having routine money habits is critical—and mostly overlooked.

Exercise: Examine your desired financial state and ask yourself these questions: What are your **specific** objectives? What are your S.M.A.R.T. (Specific, Measurable, Achievable, Realistic, Timely) goals? What is your timeframe? What is your net worth? How much monthly passive income (cash flow) do you want in relation to your expenses?

Most people have the hardest time with the "dream"—what you want it to look like, specifically, financially. This is where you will notice your "self-talk" and beliefs getting in the way. Your attention on and expectation of money will give you insight into what is important to you in relation to money.

Creating wealth requires that your intention, expectation, and attention to money *must* be in focus. You cannot make a decision about what "to do," until you know what it is you want. So, go to a beach, take a long drive, find the time to get clarity on your desired financial state. And remember, it *must* align with your vision. Be as specific as possible.

Notice that increasing income is *not* the only answer. Yet most of us grew up in a society that emphasized getting a good job, making more salary, getting good grades, and so on. Creating wealth is about financial intelligence, not scholastic aptitude. For example, did you know that the tax advantages for starting a side business far outweigh the increase in salary? Owning a business provides you with an asset, assuming you generate revenue. Your next question is: What do I do for a side business? Again, I ask you to dream—what do you want to do?

List your expenses (monthly payments for your home mortgage, car, phone, food) and liabilities (what you owe on your home, your credit cards, car loan) and notice what you are "willing" to reduce or cut.

First, if you are severely in debt, watch if your thinking is about "getting debt free." Know that not all debt is bad—you have to be smart. You have to know the rules. For those who have debt, one formula is to list all your debt in order from the highest percentage of interest owed to the lowest and create an aggressive plan to reduce the debt. Commit a specific amount of money every month to this process. Then, when you have lowered the debt, continue that same "habit" and reallocate that same amount of money to your asset column. *Do not start spending again.*

Second, if your plan includes a business (even a side business), you now have turned most of your expenses that you could never deduct as an employee to tax deductions. Your lunch out to discuss your business is now a pre-tax expense deduction, your computer and home office is now a tax-deductible expense, your vacation now includes a business meeting and is now tax deductible. Owning a business is one of the fastest ways to give yourself a raise.

Pay Attention to Your Asset Column

Now look at how you have invested in the assets. Most people have none. As Robert Kiyosaki says in *Rich Dad, Poor Dad*, "Most people have a cash flow pattern of the poor or middle class." What this looks like for the poor is all the money coming in goes out to pay expenses, and the middle class typically increases liabilities (for example, home mortgage, car payments, etc.), which increases expenses, and still they have little monthly cash flow.

The asset column is where the wealth is. This **must** become your primary financial column of interest in creating your plan. Assets that create income create wealth and passive income (this is what I call mailbox money—you do not work for it).

Current Assets	Desired Assets
Company 401K	Roth IRA (commit to annual contributions)
Cash savings	Tax deed
	Small real estate deal (producing monthly cash flow)—within three years, large real estate property.

Continue your plan of dreaming and creating. The bigger your asset column, the greater your wealth. This is where most people do not have the "capacity" or tenacity to commit to delayed gratification. The principle of compounding money in your asset column is critical. The more you put away now into investments that either produce cash flow monthly or appreciate over time such as real estate, gas wells, tax deeds, and businesses, the faster your wealth grows—through up and down cycles of the market.

I know what you are thinking: "I don't know how to invest." Neither did I! Find people to whom you aspire – not those around you who have what you have. So many of my coaching clients get advice from family, friends, or from people doing no better than they are. When I knew that I was going to become a millionaire, I knew I needed to start spending time with other millionaires. I wanted to know what they did and what their habits were. What did they read? How did they think?

Specific Strategies and Rules

There is no magic pill or script to creating wealth. Like dating, it is a committed lifestyle with increased capacity that will get you financially free and living at choice. Strategies are your action steps— what will you do, by when. They also provide accountability for your actions. Rules are the absolutes. Rules keep you true to your vision and strategy. If you think of it like a vacation, your destination is the vision, your car is the chosen strategy to get there, and road signs and maps are the rules that allow you to arrive safely.

Let me put this in personal perspective: my vision is to create financial and business literacy in the world. I have a clear picture of current and desired financial states. One of my strategies is to create a high cash flow business and then take a large portion of the revenues to invest in my asset column. Some of my rules include paying myself first, never touch any money in my asset column except to re-invest in another asset (in other words, I can't take money from my asset column to buy a boat or new car), and maintain monthly, passive cash flow greater than monthly expenses.

Your strategy could include starting a side business if you are currently an employee until the revenues are great enough for you to quit. Other options are these:

- Begin learning about real estate and how to do "no/low down deals."
- Research tax liens/deeds.
- Start your own portfolio in addition to the typical 401K (these are seen as investments and your employer controls it, so get some of your own control in your own portfolio).
- Join a network marketing company as a side business.
- Be the "deal maker" and find deals for people with money who do not have the time to look for deals.
- Make a list of strategies to support your vision to wealth. Next to it list the rules necessary to achieve it:

Strategy: Get out of debt

Rules:

- Pay a specific, consistent amount every month.
- Only use credit cards when you pay 100% of balance each month.
- Research investment so when debt is gone, the habit shifts to paying yourself first (in your asset column).

With a clear vision and a plan that has strategies and rules clearly defined, you are starting down the path. Remember this is your plan. Allow yourself to be creative and flexible. Allow yourself to "deserve" the plan and the results. In the beginning watch not to get "attached" to how it has to be—just get your intention clear that, no matter what, I deserve wealth and will have it. This is not ever at anyone's expense—this becomes a game of challenging yourself to see what your capacity is. Study those who are rich—there are very specific rules and principles. You will want these people on your team.

Your Financial Team: Who Will Help You Get There?

List the five people with whom you spend the most time. Are these people on a similar financial path? If they are not, find five others who are living the way you want. As you look for your team, consider people in the following areas: Financial Planner, Certified Public Accountant, Tax Strategist, Attorney, Real Estate Attorney, Incorporation Specialist, Millionaires—and Multi-millionaires—and those who are successful in your area of focus.

Ask these people for their support on your plan. Knowing they will support you in your journey to financial freedom is important. Getting the emotional support you need so you remain solid in your conviction to your self-vision/esteem is critically important. Have your team strategize with you. Show them the completed portions of your financial plan to explain where you are now and where you want to go.

Stay the Course

Many people search for the content, the how-to, the tips, or the magic pill. Your *choice* for financial freedom lies in your capacity to learn, grow, and reach for what you deserve. Your context is what will enable you to absorb and be able to use that information. If your self-esteem is low, if you are not truly ready to accept your financial freedom, if you cannot really see yourself there, all the content in the world will not help you achieve your goals.

Challenge yourself to grow your context by examining its origin and surrounding yourself with success. Let's face it, you've had a lifetime of financial education. You are constantly being programmed about money in print, radio, television, and now the Internet. You have little control over what you have heard in the past, but what you hear from now on and how you regard that information is within your control.

Commitment creates opportunity for action! Write that commitment, then *announce it*!

Start by writing down: "The one thing I am committed to do today is: _____.

Do this every day and share this commitment with the five people who agreed to support you on your path to financial freedom. Sharing locks in your commitment and puts it out into the world. There is no going back now. Sharing your plan and commitment engages others in your energy and your *choice* for financial freedom.

Final Thought

There is no lack of opportunity for wealth and abundance. Opportunity is unlimited. You therefore need not be competitive; it decreases you. Be creative instead! Creative increase starts with creative thought. You must focus your attention on yourself and not be concerned by what others are doing. Work on you, and let others be responsible for themselves. You must remain focused on the positives and not the negatives. This applies to thought, language, and actions. You must be grateful for all you have in order to receive more. People are naturally drawn to others who have created abundance without competition.

To Love, Light, and Wealth... Let it Flow.

About
Loral Langemeier

Loral Langemeier, M.A., C.P.P.C., is the President of Choice Performance, Inc. Loral has been a strategic coach to thousands of people since 1989 in the area of peak performance. Her areas of focus for workshops and coaching include personal responsibility, business leadership and financial impact, personal financial and investment strategies, and entrepreneurial growth.

Loral is a certified coach, author and popular speaker throughout North America and Australia. She recently began a Nationally syndicated radio show "CHOICES Live." Her personal, charismatic, bottom-line approach supports clients to get results in their business, finance, and personal life.

To contact Loral at Choice Performance, send an email to loral@choiceperformance.com, call (415) 382-8466, or visit www.choiceperformance.com.

Risk-Taking and Building Self-Esteem

by Laurie Geary

*"If you want to feel secure, do what you already know how to do.
But if you want to grow, go to the cutting edge of your competence,
which means a temporary loss of security.
So whenever you don't quite know what you are doing,
know that you are growing!"*

– Author unknown –

Taking risks builds self-esteem. Like building blocks, each risk we take contributes to a personal foundation upon which we build our self-esteem. The more blocks we have, the stronger our foundation, the more willing we are to risk, and the more able we are to handle any risks for which we are not prepared.

Webster's definition of risk—exposure to the chance of injury or loss; a hazard or dangerous chance; to imperil, jeopardize, or endanger oneself—implies that risk-taking is dangerous and thus to be avoided. Yet, the possibility of danger from risk also exposes us to the possibility of gain, success, or exhilaration. Through risk-taking, we have a chance to reach personal fulfillment and achieve our potential.

*"Self confidence comes from
the experience of having handled risk!"*

– Nathaniel Branden –

Risk-taking builds self-esteem when it is a responsible or *smart risk*, not a *foolish risk*. *Foolish risks*, such as taking drugs, eating high-fat foods, not wearing seat belts, or having unsafe sex jeopardize our health or life. Other *foolish risks* are those that we haven't prepared for, like jumping off a diving board without knowing how to swim, or investing money with no knowledge of the stock market. On the other hand, *smart risks*, such as starting a new business, learning a new skill, giving a speech, or confronting an unacceptable behavior, lead to growth and personal fulfillment. Therefore, taking risks is not something to be avoided. Rather, we need to take *smart risks* throughout our lifetime to continue to build our self-esteem.

Finding Our Growing Edge

"RISK-TAKING IS THE PATH TO PERSONAL GROWTH."

- JOSEPH ILARDO -

Taking risks requires that we move out of our *comfort zone*—a zone where our behaviors and feelings are familiar and habitual. When we leave our *comfort zone*, we move into a *learning zone*. As we learn, we grow, and thus, over time, our *comfort zone* expands to encompass our new self—with increased self-esteem. This growth process continues throughout our lifetime as we take more and more risks.

Remaining in our *comfort zone* can lead to boredom, stagnation, or even stunting of growth. All learning requires risk-taking (moving out of our *comfort zone*), and learning always builds self-esteem. Is it actually possible to remain in one's *comfort zone* and avoid risk? No, according to the Universal Law of Dissipative Structures: *The more fixed and stable something becomes, the greater the potential for instability*. So, I'd rather choose when to risk and not leave things to chance and possibly an unpleasant consequence. It is best to know how to find, and when to leave the edge of our *comfort zone*—our *growing edge*. We can prepare, prepare, prepare to risk, but there comes a point when we must stop preparing, get to our edge, and *just leap*!

"IT TAKES A LEAP OF FAITH TO GET THINGS GOING
IT TAKES A LEAP OF FAITH YOU GOTTA SHOW SOME GUTS
IT TAKES A LEAP OF FAITH TO GET THINGS GOING
IN YOUR HEART YOU MUST TRUST!"

- BRUCE SPRINGSTEEN -

The edge can be a lonely and scary place because no matter how much you prepare to risk, *you* are the only one who will make that leap off the edge into the unknown. *You* are the only one who will fully experience the consequences of your risks.

When I decided to take the biggest risk of my life—divorce after 28 years of marriage—I had to deal with all of the consequences by myself. I had to learn to live alone for the first time; I had to learn to make decisions I had never had to make before; I had to redefine my whole identity! I was completely over the edge of my comfort zone…and dealing with all the consequences alone.

There are actually two edges in our risk-taking process: the edge of our *comfort zone,* which I call our *growing edge,* and the edge of our *learning zone,* which I call our *cutting edge.* It is at our *cutting edge* where we push ourselves to our limit; this is the place where we can maximize our potential through risk-taking.

When I decided to go to graduate school, I left the edge of my comfort zone. But to maximize my potential, I had to go to the very edge of my learning zone, the cutting edge of my competence. I challenged myself to the limits of my knowledge in order to learn and grow.

Another example of being at my cutting edge is when I climb a large mountain. Once I have committed to the climb there is no going back, and I am forced to go to the cutting edge of my physical abilities— the edge of my learning zone.

Sometimes we must get to our edge before we realize what we really want. For example, you can prepare all you want to take a big risk (moving to a new location, changing jobs, getting married or divorced), but when you finally arrive at that moment of truth—the edge—you must commit to *act*, or not act. Being on the edge forces you to get in touch with what you really want. *You* must decide if you are ready to take that risk. Someone once said, "Edges are important because they define a limitation in order to deliver us from it. When we come to an edge, we come to a frontier that tells us that we are about to become more than we have been before."

For the past few years, I have been building my business as a personal and professional coach. This process has pushed me to my professional edge in so many ways: making a positive difference in so many clients' lives; becoming computer literate and creating a great website; becoming a skilled teleclass leader; designing and leading workshops; being interviewed on a radio talk show; publishing a weekly newsletter, which has led to the publication of two workbooks, this book chapter, and now another book in process. An audiotape is also in the works. I have grown so much more than I ever realized was possible. I am continually pushing my professional edge as I build my coaching business

Edges are important because they can also tell us that now is *not* the time to risk.

After my divorce, I needed to decide where to live. I seriously considered moving back to California, where I had grown up, in order to be nearer my family. So I planned and prepared to move, but at the moment I needed to make a final decision…at my edge…I realized that the move was not what I wanted to do. It took getting to my edge to clarify what I wanted. I realized it was not the time to go beyond that edge. Later I found a different edge to risk creating my new life.

Finding our edge can clarify for us what we need and want. And leaping beyond our edge can put us in the place we need to be for personal growth and fulfillment. When we are successful in our leap, our self-esteem increases!

> "PEOPLE WHO LACK SELF-ESTEEM LACK IT BECAUSE
> THEY HAVEN'T TAKEN ENOUGH RISKS!"
> - DAVID REYNOLDS -

Choosing Risk

To be successful in our risk-taking, it's best to choose our risk building blocks so that we can direct and control our personal growth. Without choice, we leave things open to chance and an outcome we don't want. Also, chance can lead to a crisis—a risk we are not prepared to handle! What do you want: A choice? Or chance and then a crisis?

When I was fourteen my mother took my sister and me to live in Spain. We attended a Catholic convent where we stayed all week, going home only on weekends. The culture shock was immense. We were not Catholic, we spoke no Spanish, and we had never lived away from home. This was a risk I did not choose, and I was definitely in crisis! Yet I learned to cope and adjust… my learning zone grew immensely. Of course, I learned fluent Spanish; but what I think I learned most was to trust that I could handle any situation. I now know with certainty that I can live anywhere and be happy.

When we choose our risks, we can be better prepared. The more we prepare for our risks, the more we maximize our opportunities for positive change and personal growth. Risk-taking moves us out of our *comfort zone* and into our *learning zone—*a transitional place where we may feel uncomfortable, confused, disoriented, even anxious—yet this zone is the only place where we learn, grow, or achieve transformational change. Because we don't like to experience these uncomfortable feelings in our *learning zone,* we often err by trying to move back into our *comfort zone*, if we can. Yet, we ought to embrace these feelings of discomfort because they signal growth. Someone once said, "You have to close one door in order to open another, but it's hell in the hallway!"

My experience in Spain may have been hell in the hallway, but many doors were opened because of it. I went on to teach Spanish, and now I do training and personal coaching in Spanish. Also, as a corporate trainer, I bring sensitivity to diversity that comes from knowing first hand what it feels like to be a minority.

We also want to have a choice in how much of a risk to take. When we take too much of a risk—go too far out of our *comfort zone*—we find ourselves in the *panic zone* rather than the *learning zone*. The *panic zone* is an area where it is difficult to learn and grow because we become emotionally flooded; we become overwhelmed by feelings of fear and anxiety and then are unable to act responsibly or rationally. All we can do is cope. There is no edge to this zone; once we are in our *panic zone,* chance of peril and hazard are at their highest.

I recently went hiking with a friend in the White Mountains of New Hampshire. We committed to climb Mt. Washington! Once above tree line, she realized she was beyond her abilities and in her panic zone, but there was no going back. Unfortunately, my friend was so flooded by feelings of fear and anxiety that she didn't grow and learn from the experience at all; she could only cope as best she could. She made it to the top, but later she said she remembered nothing of the climb.

Thus, it helps to choose the risks we want to take, and to prepare for them in order to minimize the chance of getting stuck in our *panic zone*. The *learning zone* is where we gain new skills, increase our awareness and understanding, and build our self-esteem by expanding the size of our *comfort zone* over time. In the *panic zone* we rarely learn anything.

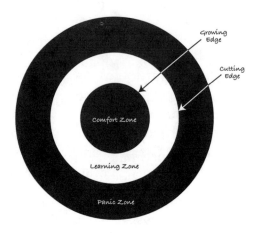

RISK PROCESS MODEL

One person's risk is not another's. Risk-taking is an individual process, thus each one of us must determine for ourselves the risks we want to take and when we want to take them. There are many different types of risks we can take: physical, emotional, financial, creative, and each of us is comfortable taking risks in certain areas.

For me, climbing Mt. Washington was not a risk. For my friend it was a risk beyond her abilities. I was prepared for that risk; she was not. On the other hand, my friend is comfortable taking emotional risks. She will risk confronting unacceptable behavior, while confrontations are risks that are difficult for me to take.

Singing in public would be a risk I would never want to take, while I love to dance in public! I have a friend who never risks dancing, but who loves to sing in front of a group.

It's best to determine for ourselves which type of risks we want to take to continue to build our risk muscle, as well as decide upon which risks will lead to our personal growth. Responsible risk-taking means having a choice based upon what is best for you.

> "THE MOST IMPORTANT INDICATOR OF HIGH MENTAL HEALTH
> IS THE WILLINGNESS TO TAKE RISKS."
> - THE CARNEGIE FOUNDATION -

The 8 A's of Responsible Risk-Taking to Build your Self-Esteem

What are all the ways we can build our self-esteem through smart risk-taking? The 8 A Risk Wheel (below) gives us a model to follow.

Each one of these A's will guide you to Risk: Achievements. Acknowledge. Affiliations. Attributes. Assertive. Authentic. Attitude. Avoid. With each **A** we need first to become **Aware** of what we need. Then we take **Action** (risk) in that area. If we set up a method for **Accountability** (like hiring a coach!) we increase our chances for success. With this process, we can **Accelerate** our self-esteem growth through responsible risk-taking.

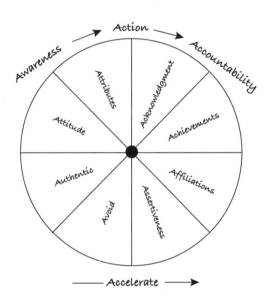

8 A's OF RESPONSIBLE RISK-TAKING

ACHIEVEMENTS

Taking stock and then keeping track of all the risks you have taken over your lifetime that have resulted in **Achievements** can contribute to a sense of pride, appreciation, and motivation to take more risks! A good exercise is for you to take your *Risk History.* List all of the risks you can remember. What happened? Who supported you? Who hindered you? What impeded you? What was the outcome? What did you learn? How did you grow? What strengths can you identify? What would you do differently next time? What would you do the same next time? The following is an example from *my Risk History:*

Risk: Outward Bound Trip
What: Eight days on a pulling boat, rock climbing, initiatives
How: 14 people

Learnings?	Strengths?	Results?
• I'm calm in a crisis	• Trustworthy	• I went on to
• I can deal with	• Dependable	become an
frustration/irritation	• Physically Fit	Outward Bound
• I am impatient with	• Coordinated	Instructor with
certain people	• Athletic	adult groups
• I am physically strong	• Supportive	• I became a role
and coordinated		model for other
• I don't want to do that again!		women
• I can push through fear		• I became a
and support others		"risk-taking" coach

Knowing that taking risks builds my *risk muscle* and therefore my self-esteem, I am now more likely to seize opportunities to risk. In the past, I may have avoided opportunities such as speaking up in a group, asking someone to dance, volunteering to participate on stage, or confronting a friend. Now, I will choose to risk knowing that I am building my self-esteem each time I risk. Then, after I risk, I acknowledge myself for my courage, and analyze what I learned, how I grew, and what I will do next time, which also helps build my self-esteem. I continue to document my *Risk History* and gain inspiration and motivation from reading it.

We build our risk muscle with our achievements by learning new skills, increasing our knowledge, and gaining new information. These all contribute to our personal growth through responsible risk-taking. There are many different types of risks we can take. We risk achievements in some of the following ways:

- Intellectually: taking or teaching courses, playing Bridge, doing crossword puzzles or mathematical equations, having intellectual discussions.
- Creatively: writing, painting, drawing, designing, singing, dancing, or acting.
- Technically: learning technical skills on the computer, getting technical training.

- Professionally: reading journals or textbooks, getting advanced training, or changing jobs.
- Physically: learning new skills: swim, ski, sail, dance, horseback ride, kayak.
- Financially: investing in or playing the stock market, investing in a new business.
- Socially: networking, committing to a new relationship, or leaving an old one.
- Emotionally: building E.Q. (emotional intelligence), expressing feelings, being authentic.
- Spiritually: going on spiritual retreats, participating in religious ceremonies.
- Culturally: traveling or living in another country, learning another language.

What type of risk-taker are you? What type do you want to develop? What type do you want to avoid?

Acknowledgment

Acknowledging ourselves for our achievements can increase our self-esteem immensely. I acknowledge myself by simply noticing what I have done (*Risk History*), then telling myself: *Well done!* Telling others of my achievements is a wonderful way to acknowledge myself. When others acknowledge us for our accomplishments, our self-esteem also increases. Unfortunately, many of us do not receive much positive feedback. Therefore, it behooves us to *ask for acknowledgment*! We should also acknowledge others as much as possible. Giving acknowledgment creates a reciprocal effect: people return compliments when they receive them. Acknowledgment is essential for building our self-esteem through risking.

Affiliations

Increasing our **Affiliations**—our connections with friends, colleagues, family, and community—and associating with those who encourage, challenge, or support us to risk is essential for successful risk-taking. Our relationships are essential to our self-esteem; they help define us. Without people in our lives, we literally cannot survive. Choosing to surround ourselves with people who will help us build our self-esteem through risk-taking, and avoiding those who discourage us, will greatly increase our chances for successful risk-taking and building our self-esteem.

I have been in a women's support group for over 5 years. Seven of us meet twice a month and share the responsibility for leading the group. We structure our sessions with rituals, readings, meditations, and poignant discussions. We've been through death, divorce, cancer, job loss, and other life transitions, and we've celebrated numerous happy occasions together. But mostly we support and encourage each other to be happy and healthy. I know my women's group has supported me in building my self-esteem over the years, and I feel filled with gratitude for their presence in my life.

Finding affiliations in **mentors and positive role models** who have successfully risked and grown can also encourage and motivate us to risk.

I have been fortunate to have many women-who-risk role models. I come from a family of strong Norwegian women who have modeled courage and independence. My mother, especially, is a wonderful risk-taker role model; she showed me how to risk and survive and succeed! As a young divorcee, she took her two teenage daughters to live and study in Spain where she became a talk radio hostess; in her 50's she became a social director on cruise ships and traveled around the world; in her early 60's she got her Ph.D. and taught in a University; in her 70's she achieved her Toastmaster Gold certificate (that's 40 speeches!), and now, in her 80's, she is self-publishing four books (one her autobiography!). She has continued to risk throughout her life and from her I know I can risk too!

You are fortunate if you have risk-taker role models in your immediate family, but you can also learn from other risk-takers. Many famous successful risk-takers have had to overcome tremendous obstacles while risk-taking. Overcoming failure and learning from it seems to be a common theme.

For example, Thomas Edison did over 2,000 experiments before he invented the light bulb. Babe Ruth is known for his home runs, but how many people know he also led the league in strike-outs? Sylvester Stallone's screen play for Rocky was rejected 19 times before he decided to produce it himself. The Beatles were turned down by Decca. Elvis Presley was fired from the Grand Ole Opry. Oprah Winfrey overcame tremendous difficulties and failures to risk her success!

We can learn a lot from risk-takers and we can be proactive in seeking them out. We can read about them or watch them in action to determine what we can learn or what we want to emulate.

Another of my risk-role models, an internationally experienced business executive, had the following to say about risk-taking:

A lot of my business life has been forcing change on people who didn't want it, and from experience I'd guess that 90% of mankind doesn't want to change anything that isn't really intolerable. After spending time with a few risk-takers—people who make a living by doing what others haven't or wouldn't (everything from real estate to base jumping)—it's clear that they focus on avoiding failure by reducing the number of things that can go wrong to nearly zero, and creating fail-safes for the rest. From personal observation the key to taking risks is setting realistic, achievable goals and time frames, and finding ways to eliminate possibilities of failure. - Carlo Zezza -

ATTRIBUTES

Developing the **Attributes** (characteristics) needed for successful risk-taking is very important. By identifying the attributes in our risk-taking role models, we can determine the characteristics we want to develop within ourselves. It is interesting to note that we have the seeds of these attributes within ourselves, or we wouldn't recognize them in others! We can only achieve what we perceive.

Successful risk-takers have the following attributes: confidence, persistence, flexibility, courage, curiosity, competence, and integrity. They have a *Can Do* attitude!

Nathaniel Branden identified six key self-esteem attributes in his book, *The Six Pillars of Self-Esteem*: Living Consciously, Living Purposefully, Self Acceptance, Self Responsibility, Self Assertiveness, and Personal Integrity.

Psychologist Abraham Maslow found that people with high self-esteem achieved self actualization: they had a zest for life, creative energy, and a good sense of humor.

Al Siebert, author of *The Survivor Personality*, found that people who survive risk-taking are playful and curious, empathic, synergistic, serendipitous, paradoxical, and intuitive.

Finding ways we can develop these attributes within ourselves will help us to be more successful in our risk-taking.

Assertive

Being **Assertive** builds our self-esteem by helping us get our needs met, while respecting the rights of others. Being assertive means taking risks by asking for what we want and rejecting what we don't want. Being assertive involves establishing personal standards (what I do want) and setting personal boundaries (what I don't want). Being assertive is risky because we may lose relationships or we may be hurt. Assertiveness, however, builds our self-esteem by clarifying our self-identity and establishing our intimate relationships. We need to learn and practice assertive skills to build our self-esteem.

Authentic

Being **Authentic** builds our self-esteem because it takes courage to be real—to be completely ourselves. We can be proud when we risk being authentic. When we are authentic, we show the world who we really are. Being authentic means being vulnerable by sharing our thoughts and feelings with others. Being authentic means being congruent with our thoughts and feelings and behaviors. Being authentic means risking intimacy. Being authentic means knowing and showing that we are special and unique; that there is no one else like us in the entire world.

> *"I AM ME.*
> IN ALL THE WORLD, THERE IS NO ONE ELSE EXACTLY LIKE ME...
> EVERYTHING THAT COMES OUT OF ME IS AUTHENTICALLY MINE
> BECAUSE I ALONE CHOOSE IT. I AM ME AND I AM OKAY."
> – VIRGINIA SATIR –

How can we become more in touch with our authentic self? Take courses in personal growth, take personal assessments, ask for feedback from others, read, observe, keep a journal and reflect on your behaviors, work with a therapist or a coach. Becoming authentic is a lifelong process: we must be willing to risk showing the world who we really are to be authentic.

Attitude

Assuming an **Attitude** that supports and encourages risk-taking for growth is essential for building your self-esteem. Attitude is everything. To risk, one needs to have a fearless attitude—a *Can Do!* attitude—a willingness to go for it! Developing positive self-talk creates an attitude that encourages us to risk. We must also become aware of, and then reduce and eliminate, any negative self-talk that discourages and keeps us from taking risks. So often, we need an *attitude adjustment*!

> "To reach our potential, we need to quiet the voice in the head that says: 'I can't do it!' "
> – Benjamin Zander –

There are many ways we can reduce our negative self-talk:

- *Cognitive Restructuring*: changing irrational beliefs into rational beliefs.
- *Thought-stopping*: stopping inner negative self talk by yelling *Stop!* in your head.
- *Jamming:* inserting positive self-talk in the place of negative self-talk.
- *Affirmations*: stating an outcome you want, as if it were true now, for example, *I am a creative and interesting writer.*
- *Visualization:* creating visual images of what you want.

Developing an **Attitude** that supports us in smart risk-taking is essential for building our self-esteem. If we *expect* to succeed when we risk, we have a greater chance of success. Our perceptions and expectations guide our actions. What we focus on is what we get. If our attitude is negative, we get negative results. If our attitude is positive, we get positive results. It is up to us. We have control of our attitude.

> "I'm convinced that...
> Life is 10% what happens to you and 90% how you react to it.
> You are in charge of your Attitudes!"
> – Charles Swindoll –

Avoid

Avoiding all the obstacles that impede us in our risk-taking and then finding ways to remove or reduce these blocks is essential to being a successful risk-taker. There are many blocks that must be removed:

- **Fear**: Fear is the biggest block to risk-taking, but fear is a natural by-product of taking risks. We encounter fear whenever we risk because we must venture out into the *unknown*. There are many types of fear that interfere with our ability and desire to risk, including fear of failure, fear of success, fear of loss, fear of conflict or adversity, fear of change, fear of rejection, fear of being disliked, fear of catastrophe, fear of intimacy or commitment, fear of the edge, even fear of fear. Yet we need to realize that when we are feeling fear we may be growing; fearful feelings signal to us that we are at our *edge* or in our *learning zone*. Fear is good: it can motivate us to act or it can motivate us to be cautious. *"Feel the Fear and Do It Anyway"* says Susan Jeffers in her book by that title. And Oprah once said, "The true meaning of courage is to be afraid. Fear is our opportunity to make shifts and transform ourselves." Fear can be a gift if you'll just open it!

  In Medieval times, all people thought that you would fall off the end of the earth at the map edge. "Here Be Dragons" would be printed at the edge of the map to indicate the unknown. Anyone who sailed over the horizon would be off to "fight their dragons." As responsible risk-takers we will need to fight our dragons…conquer our fears…in order to grow and build our self-esteem.

- **Past Negative Experiences with Risk-taking**
- **Not Enough Risk-Taking**
- **Poor Support System or Few Role Models**
- **Lack of Motivation:** Use the 8 A's of Responsible Risk-taking to get motivated!
- **Lack of Reserves of Money, Time, Energy, Support:** Reserves are necessary to support us in order to risk successfully; find ways to build up reserves to be fully prepared.
- **Age:** Our life stages often determine whether we are ready to risk or not; we take different risks at different ages.

- **Timing:** This may not be the *right time* to take a risk. Or you may not have *enough time* to take a risk. In this case, you must find and use time management techniques and other ways to simplify your life in order to create the time needed to risk.

- **Unmet Needs:** If we have unmet needs, moving forward and taking risks is difficult. Psychologist Abraham Maslow identified our basic needs as physiologic (water, oxygen, food, sleep, health), needs for safety and security, social needs, and achievement needs. These needs must be satisfied in a hierarchical manner. According to his theory, we won't be able to risk achievement (level #4) or reach self-actualization (level #5) if we are sick or hungry (level #1). Identifying and then satisfying our lower level (physical and psychological) needs is important before we can take that leap to risk.

- **Lack of Information, Knowledge, or Skill**

- **Poor Preparation:** Prepare by following the *3-Step Risk-Taking Process* (see next section).

- **Habits:** Our habits keep us in our *comfort zone* and keep us from wanting to risk. Changing habits can be very difficult. To change we must first create an intention to change, then establish and practice a new routine to develop a new habit. Another effective method is to attach a new habit to an old habit and then: repetition, repetition, repetition! Neurophysiology research has proven that we can create new passageways in our brains to create new habits. We know that if we keep doing what we're doing, we're going to keep getting what we're getting!

- **Cultural Conditioning:** People are influenced by their cultures; certain cultures are more likely to risk than others. For example, Americans may be more likely to risk since our ancestors were adventurers and pioneers.

- **Familial Scripting:** Our birth order, family experiences, and family messages will all influence our ability and desire to risk. We need to examine and question our scripting to determine if it's a script we still want to follow.

- **Genetic Coding:** Studies have found that some people have genes that predispose them to risk, or not to risk. Psychologist

Frank Farley identified the *little t/Big T personalities*. People with *Big T(hrill)* need to take big risks often; *little t(hrill)* people were happy in their *comfort zone*. Another study found a novelty-seeking gene: people with this gene risk to find novelty; they're not happy remaining in their *comfort zone*. Paul Stoltz, author of *The Adversity Quotient,* found three types of people in his research: *Quitters, Campers, Climbers. Quitters* are people who need very little exposure to risk to be happy; *Campers* risk some, but then find their *comfort zone* to camp out in; *Climbers* are the people who continue to risk throughout their lifetime. The good news is that these experts found that our genetic coding can be altered by experience.

- **Gender Expectations:** Women are traditionally not encouraged to risk as much or as often as men, for many reasons: cultural conditioning, family scripting, not enough role models, as well as not as many opportunities to risk. Studies have found that women fear success, they learn helplessness, and they must deal with a *Glass Ceiling*. In general, women have difficulty risking being Assertive and making Achievements. Fortunately, many of these obstacles to women's risk-taking are being reduced. Women are getting much more involved in athletic activities and they are moving into leadership roles in business, politics, and academics, so they have more opportunities to risk. History books and fairy tales are being rewritten to represent more of women's contributions, so there are more risk-taking role models.

    Men, on the other hand, have difficulty taking emotional risks; they fear being emotionally vulnerable and have trouble risking intimacy and commitment. Men have difficulty risking being Authentic.

    Men and women can learn from each other to counteract gender expectations that impede risking for self-esteem growth.

- **Tolerations:** Tolerations are events, people, situations, stuff you put up with that drain your energy—anything that keeps you from being yourself and from taking risks. Tolerations are like holes in your personal success cup—no matter how much you put into the cup, the toleration-hole lets it all drain out. Then you have no energy to risk. Tolerations are found in all aspects of our life: home, office, relationships, family, clients, customers, pets, car, appliances, equipment, body, appearance, and much more. The first step in reducing your tolerations is to recognize *what* you are tolerating. A torn curtain or shirt? A dirty car or house? A messy closet or desk? An unfinished letter or conversation? A chronically-late friend? First identify, then *zap* those tolerations! The benefits of reducing or eliminating tolerations are many: you will feel freer, have more energy, become more creative, attract better opportunities, strengthen yourself, and enjoy life more. You will be plugging those holes in your personal success cup so that you can be more successful in whatever you do and be able to take more risks to build your self-esteem!

Identifying and then finding ways to **Avoid** blocks to your risk-taking process in order to build your self-esteem is extremely important. What are your blocks?

Note: For a more detailed list of all the obstacles to risk-taking, see my workbook: *Risk to Grow: Create the Life You Want through Responsible Risk-taking*, which also includes assessments, exercises, top tens, quotes and poems, a comprehensive list of resources, and much more.

Personal Risk Assessment

We build our self-esteem by taking an assessment of each of the **8 A's of Responsible Risk-Taking.** First, it helps to become **Aware** of our need to risk in each of the **8 A-areas.** By using the Risk Wheel, we can do a personal assessment to determine which area we want to develop and then what actions we need to take.

Directions: On a scale of 1-10, with 1 being in the center of the wheel and 10 being the outer edge of the wheel, determine where you are with regards to each of the A's. How much are you in balance? What areas do you need to develop to get more in balance? How will you do that?

The following is an example of a personal risk wheel assessment:

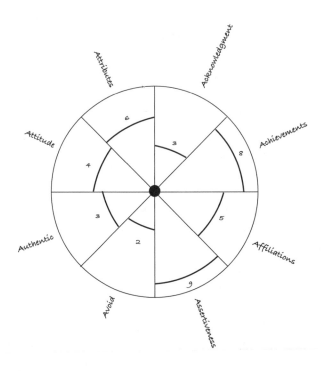

PERSONAL RISK ASSESSMENT WHEEL

The 3-Step Risk-Taking Process:
Create - Commit - Complete

STEP ONE - CREATE

Create wth the **3 R's: Readiness-Rehearsal-Relaxation**

A. Readiness

Key Questions to ask yourself (and answer):
- What are the possible/expected consequences of taking this risk?
- What will be the potential **Gains? (Pros)** What will be the **Costs? (Cons)**

- What's the **worst** possible consequence? What is the **best** possible consequence? (Could I handle these consequences?)
- Who is part of my **support system**?
- Whom should I avoid (non-supportive/toxic people)?
- Whom should I add to my relationship connections?
- How will this risk affect the people in my life?
- What are my responsibilities? What responsibilities will others have?
- Who are my **role models/mentors**? What can I learn from them?
- What **skills** do I need to learn? What **information/education** do I need?
- What are my **Goals**? Are they **S.M.A.R.T** (Specific, Measurable, Achievable, Realistic, Trackable)?
- What's my **Plan**? What are my **Action Steps**? Have I prioritized my **Action** steps?
- Is this the right time to take this risk? Will I regret it if I don't take this risk now?
- How will I feel later (XX years from now) not having taken this risk? Do I have enough time to take this risk? What can I eliminate/delegate in order to have time?
- Do I have a strong enough **personal foundation** (self-esteem) to take this risk now?
- Do I have the **reserves** (of time, money, energy, health, support...) I need to take this risk?
- What are my **blocks** to taking this risk? How can I reduce/eliminate them?
- How can I **motivate** myself to take this risk?
- What's my *gut* feeling/intuition about taking this risk?
- Do I have the **characteristics (attributes)** of a *smart* risk-taker? How can I develop them?
- Can I create an **environment** that will motivate, encourage, support me in risk-taking?
- Can I develop a **child's point of view** to take this risk? How can I play and risk?
- Do I **trust** myself to handle the risk and risk consequences? Do I **trust** the Risk Process?

- Can I create a **safety net** for this risk? Is there a way I can *go back* if the risk doesn't work?

B. Rehearsal

- Role play: Practice the risk ahead of time (if possible).
- Think *As If*...Feel *As If*...Act *As If*: *Fake it 'til you make it!*
- Take mini-steps to test out the risk.
- Write out your *risk plan.*
- Discuss your risk plan with supportive friends/colleagues.
- AudioTape/VideoTape your risk.
- Visualize successfully having achieved this risk.

C. Remember Relaxation

Learn and practice diaphragmatic breathing techniques before and during risk-taking. Learn anxiety reduction techniques such as systematic relaxation, deep muscle relaxation, meditation, creative visualization, and yoga to prepare yourself for taking your risk.

STEP TWO: COMMIT

A. Action! Take that risk - Go for it!

B. Maintain your Commitment: Do what you need to do to keep yourself in your Risk Learning Zone. Take care of yourself (eat well, sleep well, exercise, relax, meditate, stay focused), be persistent, and have courage!

C. Trust in the risk process: Trust in the *8 A's of Responsible Risk-taking.* Trust yourself. Trust in the Universe: *The moment one definitely commits oneself, providence moves too.*

STEP THREE: COMPLETE

A. Evaluate the *success* of your risk—what did you achieve? What did you learn? What would you do differently next time? The risk-taking process is like a cycle that is constantly moving and ever-changing. What do you need to do now?

B. Celebrate! Reward yourself for risk-taking! *Tah dah!*

C. Next Steps: **Ask Yourself**: what is the **next step** in this risk? or what **new risk** do I want to take next? What big risk could I take now that would substantially improve the quality of my life? What risks can I take to continue to build my self-esteem?

In Conclusion

Using the **8 A's of Responsible Risk-taking** can greatly increase your ability to build your self-esteem throughout your lifetime. We build our self-esteem with our **Achievements**. We build our self-esteem when we **Acknowledge** ourselves for risk-taking and when we ask others to acknowledge us. We build our self-esteem as we develop positive **Attributes** to help us take responsible risks. We build our self-esteem as we use our **Affiliations** to support and encourage us to risk. We build our self-esteem when we risk being **Authentic**. We build our self-esteem when we develop an **Attitude** that encourages us to risk. We build our self-esteem when we are **Assertive** to assure successful risk-taking. We build our self-esteem by identifying, and then **Avoiding** our blocks to smart risk-taking. With each **A,** we must first become **Aware** of the action we need to take to build our self-esteem. Then we take **Action** using a method of **Accountability**. By following the **8 A's of Responsible Risk-taking** we **Accelerate** our self-esteem growth. Finally, by following **the 3-Step Model for Responsible Risk-taking**, we create the best opportunity for building our self-esteem through risk-taking!

"IF YOU CANNOT RISK, YOU CANNOT GROW
IF YOU CANNOT GROW, YOU CANNOT BECOME YOUR BEST.
IF YOU CANNOT BECOME YOUR BEST, YOU CANNOT BE HAPPY.
IF YOU CANNOT BE HAPPY, WHAT ELSE MATTERS?"

- DAVID VISCOTT -

"UNTIL ONE IS COMMITTED, THERE IS HESITANCY,
THE CHANCE TO DRAW BACK, ALWAYS INEFFECTIVENESS.
CONCERNING ALL ACTS OF INITIATIVE THERE IS ONE ELEMENTARY TRUTH,
THE IGNORANCE OF WHICH CALLS COUNTLESS IDEAS AND SPLENDID PLANS:
THAT THE MOMENT ONE DEFINITELY COMMITS ONESELF,
PROVIDENCE MOVES TOO. ALL SORTS OF THINGS OCCUR TO
HELP ONE THAT WOULD HAVE NEVER OCCURRED.
A WHOLE STREAM OF EVENTS ISSUES FROM THE DECISION,
RAISING IN ONE'S FAVOR ALL MANNER OF UNFORESEEN INCIDENTS
AND MEETINGS AND MATERIAL ASSISTANCE WHICH NO MAN COULD
HAVE DREAMT WOULD HAVE COME HIS WAY.
WHATEVER YOU CAN DO, OR DREAM YOU CAN, **BEGIN IT!**
BOLDNESS HAS GENIUS, POWER, AND MAGIC IN IT."

- GOETHE -

COACHING QUESTIONS

- What risks do you need to take now? How can you keep building your risk muscle?
- What type of risk-taker are you? Do you want to change your type? How will you do that?
- What risk could you take now that would profoundly change your life?
- What small risks can you take now that will make a difference later on?
- What risks do you regret not having taken?
- What risks have you taken in your life? What did you learn? What strengths did you identify within yourself? (Take your *Risk History*.)
- What are all your *Achievements*? What are you most proud of achieving?
- In what ways do you *Acknowledge* yourself for risking? Do you acknowledge yourself publicly? Do you ask for acknowledgment? Do you regularly give acknowledgement?
- Who are your *Affiliations*? Who is your strongest support? How can you build your support system? Who are your role models/mentors?
- How *Assertive* are you (on a scale of 1-10)? What do you need to do to become more assertive?
- What do you need to do to adjust your *Attitude* for more successful risk-taking?
- What blocks/obstacles do you need to A*void* in order to be more successful risking?
- How can you become more *Authentic*?
- How will you use the *3-Step Risk-Taking Model* to be successful in your risk-taking?

Bibliography/Resources:

BOOKS

Branden, Nathaniel. *The Six Pillars of Self-esteem*. New York: Bantam Books, 1994.

Canfield, Jack. *Self-esteem & Peak Performance*. Audio cassette. Career Track, 1991.

Covey, Stephen. *The 7 Habits of Highly Effective People*. New York: Simon & Schuster, 1989.

DiClemente, Carl, John Norcross and James Prochaska. *Changing for Good*. New York: Avon Books, 1994.

Gawain, Shakti. *Creative Visualization*. San Rafael, CA: Whatever Publishing, 1978.

Ilardo, Joseph. *Risk-Taking for Personal Growth: A Step-by-Step Workbook*. Oakland, CA: New Harbinger Press, 1992.

Jeffers, Susan. *Feel the Fear and Do It Anyway*. New York: Balantine Books, 1987.

Jones, Barbara Schindler and Betty Morscher. *Risk-Taking for Women*. New York: Everest House, 1982.

Marone, Nicky. *Women & Risk: A Guide to Overcoming Learned Helplessness*. New York: St. Martin's Press, 1992.

O'Brien, Virginia. *Success on Your Own Terms: Tales of Extraordinary, Ordinary Business Women.* New York: Wiley & Sons, 1998.

Satir, Virginia. *Self-esteem.* Celestial Arts, 2001.

Siebert, Al. *The Survivor Personality.* New York: Berkley Publishing, 1996.

Simon, Sidney. *Getting Unstuck: Breaking through your Barriers for Change.* Warner Books, 1989.

Stoltz, Paul. *Adversity Quotient: Turning Obstacles into Opportunities.* New York: John Wiley & Sons, 1997.

Viscott, David. *Risking.* New York: Simon & Schuster, 1977.

Zander, Benjamin and Rosamund Stone. *The Art of Possibility.* Boston, MA, 1999.

JOURNALS

Holes in Those Genes. Newsweek. January 15, 1996.

The Big T(hrill) Personality: Why Some Like It Hot. Working Woman. February, 1990.

PLACES TO BUILD YOUR RISK MUSCLE

Hurricane Island Outward Bound School: P.O. Box 429, Rockland, ME 04841 (800-341-1744)

Project Adventure: P.O. Box 100, Hamilton, MA 01936 (800-796-9917)

Toastmasters International: P.O. Box 9052, Mission Viejo, CA 92690 (714-858-8255)

National Speakers Association: 1500 S. Priest Drive, Tempe, Arizona (480-968-2552)

Jack Canfield Self-Esteem Seminars: www.chickensoupforthesoul.com

International Coach Federation: 1444 "I" St. NW-Suite 700, Washington, D.C, 20005 (888-423-3131)

About
Laurie Geary

As a Personal and Professional Coach, Laurie draws upon her Masters in Psychological Education, her (over 20) years of experience as a teacher (High School English and Spanish), and trainer (for Professional Organizations and Community Groups on Self Esteem Building, Assertiveness Training, Conflict Resolution, Effective Communication Skills, Responsible Risk-Taking, Stress Management, Parent Education, Team Building, and more.). She leads teleclasses on Risk-taking, Finding Your Passion, Building your Self Esteem, and more. She also utilizes her skill as an instructor for Outward Bound to encourage clients to take responsible risks in order to grow and evolve to create the life they want. Fluent in Spanish, Laurie also offers coaching and training for Spanish-speaking clients.

She is a graduate of the University of Virginia (B.S.), Boston University (M.Ed.), and Coach University. She is a Professional Certified Coach (P.C.C.) and a Certified Teleclass Leader; Laurie has been coaching for over 5 years. She uses a number of assessment tools with her clients, and, as a certified administrator of the Myers-Briggs Type Indicator (MBTI), she offers trainings as well as individual interpretation/coaching to her clients.

Originally from southern California, Laurie lived in Europe (Spain and Germany) during her high school years. She attended college in Virginia (Mary Washington College and then the University of Virginia); and graduate school in Boston (Boston University).

After teaching high school, Laurie became an adult educator as an instructor for a number of companies, such as the Teacher Education Institute, the American Management Association, Forum, and Lee Hecht Harrison. Laurie was also a Director of Community Education (at a Mental Health Center), a leader for the Appalachian Mountain Club's Mountain Leadership School, and facilitator for Outward Bound Professional programs. As President of *In Gear*